Insecure and Confident

Tamara Filch

Copyright © 2024 by Tamara Filch

All rights reserved.

No portion of this book may be reproduced in any form without written permission from the publisher or author, except as permitted by U.S. copyright law.

Contents

1. CHAPTER 1: My Boys — 1
2. Chapter 2: Blane's Party — 5
3. CHAPTER 3: Ric's girlfriend — 10
4. CHAPTER 4: Sleepover — 14
5. CHAPTER 5: She left — 19
6. CHAPTER 6: housemate — 24
7. CHAPTER 7: Broken windows — 30
8. CHAPTER 8: Not so rude Blane — 36
9. CHAPTER 9: Sleepover at Blane's — 42
10. CHAPTER 10: Accidents — 49
11. CHAPTER 11: After Accidents — 55
12. CHAPTER 12: Old Memories — 62
13. CHAPTER 13: No longer Secrets — 67
14. CHAPTER 14: Oblivious Victoria — 73
15. CHAPTER 15: Happy State — 79

16. CHAPTER 16: All good until   84
17. CHAPTER 17: Spa   91
18. CHAPTER 18: Carnivals   97
19. CHAPTER 19: Not just friends   102
20. CHAPTER 20: Parents   108
21. CHAPTER 21: Strawberries   115
22. CHAPTER 22: New discoveries   121
23. CHAPTER 23: Logan Martinez   126
24. CHAPTER 24: Bye Ric   131
25. CHAPTER 25: Bake   136
26. CHAPTER 26: News   141
27. CHAPTER 27: Second chance   147
28. CHAPTER 28: Bella   152
29. CHAPTER 29: ART   157
30. CHAPTER 30: Connecting   163
31. CHAPTER 31: Butt   171
32. CHAPTER 32: Drinks   178
33. CHAPTER 33: hanging   185
34. CHAPTER 34: Dress up   192
35. CHAPTER 35: Business Woman   198
36. CHAPTER 36: Puppy Blane   202
37. CHAPTER 37: Family   207
38. CHAPTER 38: Not just one   212

39. CHAPTER 39: Saint John industries   218

40. CHAPTER 39: Father Daughter   223

41. CHAPTER 40: Beach   230

42. CHAPTER 41: Perfect   235

43. CHAPTER 42: Never been my mother   241

44. CHAPTER 43: I'll see you soon   249

45. CHAPTER 44: Anywhere but home   255

46. CHAPTER 45: Prom night   261

47. CHAPTER 46: I Promise   271

CHAPTER 1: My Boys

*************For as long as i could remember i was referred to as fat but i rather go by thick with a little bit of flab on my arms and my stomach. Anyway i didn't actually care what the people in school think i was pretty confident about myself, at least that's what I let everyone believe. I didn't care cause my family still loved me regardless and my four best friends loved me a lot and always made me feel comfortable with who i am.

My best friends all boys and i wound not have preferred it any other way. Eric and Ian who were my neighbours literally next door, we practically grew up together. They were twins but not the kind that looked alike they were complete opposites of each other, Ric was always sweet and calm but Iano, I decided to call him that cause Ian sounded so boring but Iano had a certain ring to it but he never let anyone else call that except of course me, he was cocky and never missed an opportunity to flirt. Brian we met him in kindergarten and he just fit right into our little group. Frank was a new student from Germany who moved to America cause his parents got a job here. He pronounced English words funny which made us crack up that's how he slowly became part of our family too.

I got up to school I usually walk to school its like a thirty minute walk and It made me feel like i exercise everyday I don't say that out loud though.

"Hey Tony over here"

Without even lifting my head up to see who called I immediately knew it was Iano he decided to call me Tony my full name is Victoria Martinez but he said Tony was more one of the boys as he put it I liked it though. When I got to where they were I said hello and they all took my hand and kissed it was their idea not mine they said they wanted to feel like a queen and queens always had their hands and I thought it was the most stupid thing they thought of but I liked it a lot. I turned my attention back to my phone and kept scrolling through instagram's explore page. Suddenly Frank took my phone and ran into the school's hallway and I got up trying to get to him while the rest laughed as I ran. i wasn't even close to frank when I tripped on something but when I raised my head to see Gwen laughing with her two friends. Ric quickly helped me up and asked if i was okay and pulled me aside just when i wanted to tear this bumblehead's ass up.

"okay look Gwen I don't care who the hell you think you are but if you try to act stupid around Victoria so help me God you will regret it and that's a promise i will keep" Iano said

I looked at Gwen who was clearly hurt since she has a crush on Iano for the longest but he pays her no mind. I could see the anger In her eyes as she walked off and the two bafoons followed her like lost puppies. Brian handed me my bag and I asked them to tell Frank I needed my phone after class.

I headed to class alone cause we rarely had class together i was brighter than all of them combined so I always helped them out studying for tests and what not. I got to class and sat in my usual sit somewhere near the back but the not the back. I sat alone not talking to anyone as I thought of how this was my last year and I would no longer have to deal with people like Gwen which gave me great comfort. I saw Blane come in but didn't go to his usual back seat instead he sat next to me he was attractive but i didn't like him anymore. I remember the time I developed a crush on him cause he defended me when i was being picked on and my boys weren't around but that was a long time ago in the fourth grade I think. I got over my crush when his friends picked on me but just watched, if anything he laughed a little bit. He was staring I could his glare on me which made me very uncomfortable.

"Can I help you with something?"

"Did I say I needed anything"

I rolled my eyes when the teacher got in I ignored his presence and listened to everything being said. when class was over he was still staring so I quickly packed up my stuff and got up and left among the first people leaving the class. I saw Frank talking to some girl I think she is new cause I had never seen her. I could tell he was flirting with her and this was the perfect opportunity to enact my revenge.

"Hey baby you said you would text me last after you left why didn't you?" by the time i was done saying that one sentence in the most seductive way I could think of she walked away looking all disgusted.

"Why would you do that Tony,she was an 8"

I rolled my eyes and told him to hand over my phone he did and ran after his 8.

When my last class was finished I went straight to the parking lot cause the boys and I always had a smoothie after school together then dropped me home as they went to do whatever they do on Mondays. I got home and had watched my favourite show FRIENDS.

I had my dinner went to my bedroom brushed up on my chemistry and went to bed.

****

Chapter 2: Blane's Party

**********************

"So Tony, Blane is hosting a party at his house, You should come you know loosen up a little"

I stared at Iano as if he had just said the most absurd thing anyone would say to me.

"Come on Tony we'll be with you the whole time we will even bring you back home please come with us" I was about to refuse and tell them i rather just watch FRIENDS and eat popcorns until Iano said "Come one Tony I dare you or are too scared of stupid cheerleaders"

I got up from where i sat and tried to get him so that I smack his head but who are kidding i couldn't catch him. " You know what i will go to Blane's stupid party cause am not scared of some stupid bubblehead cheerleader"They rolled their eyes at tge sometimes you'll think they planed it.

The party was in a few hours they left my house and said they come around seven to pick me up. I was in the bath tub when I realised I just had twenty minutes to get ready which was more that I needed. I never put on make up like the other school girls not that i didn't try am just not gifted in that form of art. I put on my black reliable trousers and Brian's hoody that I loved. when i was ready I went downstairs to tell my mom i will be out late.

"Hey mom am going out with my boys I might come back at around ten its cool right"

My mom just laughed like she always did when I referred to the guys as my boys.

"Sure hunny just don't come home drunk, say hello to your boys for me"

I heard a honk from outside and that was my que to get out I took breathe and headed toward Ric and Iano's jeep. they got it for their sixteenth birthday. I got into the front passenger seat cause that was my seat. Ric was driving he was more of a responsible driver so i was not worried today.

"my mom said she missed you guys"

"You mean our mom, we miss her too how about we come for a sleepover on Tuesday"

I rolled my eyes it was a habit of mine and told him sure they all agreed to come to the sleepover on Tuesday. I knew my mom missed them cause they practically lived in our house well till the senior year stress. We agreed on Tuesday cause we usually didn't have that much homework. We got to Blane's house and his house was beautiful I knew they were loaded but I just thought normal loaded not mansions and huge pools loaded. My boys started shouting and waving at some of their friends i walked quietly behind them when we got into the house it was beautiful the colour, the furniture all shouted rich. the music was too loud for my liking but it was a party Ric brought me a drink and sat next to me i decided to sit somewhere in the garden cause most people were in or around the pool. Iano was now flirting with some girl who looked older than him but he didn't seem to mind. Frank was talking to the girl from the time I extracted my revenge I smiled at the memory of the girl walking off. Brian was dancing with a girl i think they were in the same class she was pretty they looked cute.

"So Ric why aren't you dancing with you some random girl" he laughed revealing his left side dimple.

"Because Tony,"

"I don't think my girlfriend would like me dancing with some random girl"

I couldn't believe what I just heard my Ricky had a girlfriend and I didn't know about it. I didn't think anyone knew about it. so obviously I asked him so many questions he decided to leave pretending he had to go the bathroom. but I found out her name was Eva he even showed me a picture she was blonde and very pretty. but that's all I got.

When i was alone I decided why not tour this mansion. So i got up and started walking around. I noticed a room with a red door that said do not enter which obviously made me intrigued. So i did what any other would do in my situation find out what was in the room. I looked around to seeif anyone was watching and I quickly opened the door that was not locked. I got in and closed the door behind me. It was not what i expected. It was a home theatre this seven comfortable red seats. I sat down and I saw a remote control I pressed play and i saw a video tape of a woman just from bath but she looked unconscious and a man I recognized. He was Blane's dad well when he was younger he was cute. He held a baby who was crying I think it was Blane I got up to take a closer look when I heard someone get in.

"Did you not understand the sign outside Martinez"

I turned around and saw Blane looking extremely furious and I couldn't think of an excuse to give him so I kept quiet. he started walking towards me and stopped when he was standing intimidatingly in front of me. He looked at me as if i was something not worth being looked.

"Leave"

I didn't move how could I when he was standing so close to me I had to hold my breathe.

"I said GET OUT"

I immediately came to my senses and got out as fast I could. I got ot and went to look Ric cause I really wanted to go home. But thanks to my awful I met the devil herself. Se was me try to go the opposite direction which made her call out my name. I was honestly not in the mood for her BS.

"What do want Gwen?" I asked obviously pissed off

"Well, you see i didn't appreciate Ian's tone when he spoke to me the other day so how would you like to go for a swim"

Next thing I knew her two puppies were dragging me to the pool area as people stared and laughed. I clearly understood what she mean by would I like to go for a swim but I would not go in alone so when the tried to push me into the pool fully clothed I grabbed on to the two puppies and we all fell in. I was that good of a swimmer. when i was in the pool I realised t was not the shallow end it was so deep I couldn't feel the bottom of the pool. Someone grabbed me and help me to the shallow end and i was breathing really quick trying to catch my breathe. I didn't know who helped me until he dragged me to what I presume was his room. Blane, still very much angry he even got angrier if it was possible.

my clothes were all wet and dripping. He went to his closet and handed me probably his largest sweatpants and a large shirt.

"You can change into that the bathroom is over there"

Before i could even thank him he left and i went into the bathroom and changed into his sweatpants they were tight they showed off my curves an

I loved the shirt. when I got out of his room I saw Ric. He came rushing towards me and asked i was okay. I told him i was okay I just wanted to go home. Ric drove me home, he wanted to come in and make sure am okay but I told him i wanted to be alone so he went back to the party to pick up the other guys. I ignored my Mom when they tried to talk me and locked myself in my room . I sat on my bed and Watched FRIENDS on my laptop soom enough i was asleep.

CHAPTER 3: Ric's girlfriend

∧ ^^ A PICTURE OF EVA....^^^^

************Sunday literally flew by. My boys called me and asked if i was okay Iano wanted to come by, am guessing he felt guilty cause he wasn't there for me but i didn't blame him for what happened.

I couldn't help but think about the tape of Blane's mother I presume she looked lifeless but Blane does have a mom. His parents always donated huge amounts of money whenever we had charity events but i have never seen them. I saw his Dad once but he was not with his wife. Why did Blane help me if he was still angry with me? It was all so weird maybe he is not that bad of a person as I thought.

I really was not in the learning mood but my parents wouldn't let me just skip school so I had no other option but to go. I was close to school I could see the parking lot I stood and took deep breaths, its not like that was my first embarrassing incident i have been through a lot trust me but I don't know why this one felt different. My boys saw me from their usual spot they all stood up and came running, they all hugged me I loved the group hugs cause am always in the middle and it made me feel protected they started tickling me and i couldn't hold in my laughter. As we all laughed I could see people pass as by and look at as but I just brushed it off.

"I know something that will cheer you up"

He told me that after I left after the incident Blane told Gwen and her puppies to leave and they were no longer invited to his parties. I was happy cause he did that because of me but I didn't put much thought into it. we all headed to our different classes. My first class was with Blane. He came in and sat next to me like did the other time but this time he didn't acknowledge my presence. He seemed angry about something.

"Hey Blane"

He didn't even spare me a glance he kept on looking at the ceiling.

"I just wanted to say thank you for saving when i was thrown into the pool, I don't know how to swim i would have drowned...."

He still didn't move you'd think i never existed. I decided to leave him alone when the teacher came in. I kept looking at him from time to time but he still ignored me.

************During Lunch I sat with my boys as usual it was pizza day amd who didn't like pizza except for Ric but i ate his piece. Everyone was on their phones when i suddenly remembered about Ric's girlfriend."I know a secret y'all should probably know" They all kept their phones down but i kept quiet and ate my pizza, tgey all looked but i ignored them and kept on eating."Come on, stop teasing and tell us already" Brian said.I laughed " okay so".....I took another bite of my pizza as the groaned."Okay Okay.... Ric has a girlfriend called Eva"I felt Ric stiffened next to me. They all turned to Ric for answers. He groaned loudly and looked me as i laughed at him.

"Okay,...Her name is Eva but you already know that what do you want to know??"

We huddled up so that we all didn't speak at once. I came up with the idea for us to huddle up whenever we had many questions but we want only one person to ask so that it's confusing for the one we are questioning. Frank was always the one to ask the questions. We dissolved the huddle when we were done.

"Where does she go to this school?"

"No, she is in a different city its a long distance thing..."

"How old is she?"

"17.. turning 18 this summer.."

"Have you too ever met?"

"Not recently, but we used to be talk from waaay back and we get along well"

"Okay the last and most important question .... do you really like her or its just for fun?"

He signed heavily and then smiled

"Yes i really like and i actually think its very serious for both us.."

"Ooooouuuuuuuhhhh" we all said in a girlish voice making him roll his eyes the he just laughed. I was very happy for him since he not always that interested in girl which made really want to meet Eva.

**************When school was over i went to the parking lot and the boys were already there ao i got in and we went to the smoothie hut. We stayed there for about two hours then they dropped me i reminded them about the sleepover and they said they were still coming. When i got home i told my mom abozr the sleepover and she was happy she even said she was going to make dinner.

****

CHAPTER 4: Sleepover

∧ ^^^^A PICTURE OF FRANK^^^^^^

***************We heading home from the smoothie hut for the sleepover i was pretty excited cause we haven't had one of these in a long time. When we got in my mom literally was over joyed she hugged them as if she had not seen her children in a year.

"Ric, Sweetheart your so thin have not been taking care of yourself?"

We all laughed when he said she never sent him cookies anymore thats why. Yes my mom used to send them cookies every weekend in a huge container and the loved them.

"Good thing i made some for all of you. Okay come one diner is ready its almost 8 "

We all gathered around the table and my mom had made the boys favourite, lasagna. Apparently it was the best they ever ate, i thought it was just okay. We ate as mom kept asking them questions of how have been and about school. When we were done i helped clean the utensils while the boys played video games in the living room. I went to living room when i was done helping out. She said she was heading out to see her friend who works alot and isn't around much.

Later on when we went to my bed we randomly started talking about life but i noticed Frank was quiet it wasn't like him he would have joked about something by now.

"Hey Frank, are you alright?"

The rest turned to look at him he looked worried.

"Yeah its just my parents....." He trailed off.

"What's happened, i hope they are okay?"

"They are okay health wise but they're getting a divorce apparently they have been having problems for a long time..."

"OMG... Am so sorry Frank we had no idea"

I got up and gave him a hug while the guys told him it will be alright. Iano joked about him having two birthday parties from each parent.

"My mom will be going back to Germany but my dad will stay back here so i will be spending my holidays with my mom but i have to stay here cause its my senior year.."

He added. I was happy he didn't have to leave cause i would have really missed him. But i know he was really fond of his mom than his Dad. We lightened the mood with music from the 90's i made them listened to it music cause i loved them, they also did but i was not allowed to tell anyone. Boys.

My mom had put out a mattress on the floor for the boys. Iano slept on the bed with me though cause he says his skin is too pretty to be anywhere near the ground. In the middle of the night he would suddenly spoon me i used to think it was wierd but i got used to it so i didn't think much of it. Ric, Frank and Brian were on the mattress while Iano and i were on the bed.

"Do you think we would still be close like this and have sleepovers when all of you have girlfriends?" I asked

They all looked at me as if i asked them a very hard question.

"Well,, I told Eva about you and how close we are and about the sleepovers. She didn't seem to mind. I told her your like a sister to me and she's cool with it as long you try don't anything.."

I laughed at what Ric said the part about me trying something. But i liked Eva more she seemed cool because most girlfriends don't even want their boyfriends having a female friend.

"I like her already" i said to Ric. I looked at the others "what about you guys?"

"You can try something with me.." Iano looked at me with smirk then winked.

"Eeeew, come on i rather try something with Frank your a Man hoe."Iano placed his hand on his chest as if i just said the most absurd thing he has ever heard acting shocked. We all laughed.

"You don't have to worry about me.."Brian said brushing off the issue.

"We will definitely stay close you were my first friend when i came to school on my first day and i wouldn't just throw that away we are definitely staying close."

"Aaaaaw group hug" They groaned and jumped on me making me laugh as i tried to push they off me.

"Okay we better sleep we still have school tomorrow. Goodnight Boys"

We said goodnight and slept.

****

Wednesday morning i was pretty tired cause we slept at around 1. I used my moms bathroom while the boys used mine. My mom still wasn't back from yesterday she texted me telling me she would just sleep at her friend's place. I made pancakes for the boys and after breakfast we left the house heading to school.

Mr. lorence, our math teacher, was very petty he saw me dozed off and gave me detention. Great. All the detentions i ever had were administered by him. After all my classes i headed to detention it was empty no one was in there so it was going to be just me and mr. Lorence.

I took out my Bio book to go through what was taught today cause i think i just heard half of it. On my second page of the chapter i heard the door open and Blane came in. He looked at me with a raised eyebrow and came and sat near me. He was in a good mood it seemed.

"Hey Martinez,"

"Hy"

"So what you doing here,"

"Ooh you know i just thought why not hang out with Mr. Lorence for an hour."

He smirked " it's just not really your scene..."

"I can be a bad girl "

He laughed and that's when i realized how kinky that sounded, ooh i have been a bad girl.

"Thank you for what you did the other day... You know saving me from drowning" I said trying to changing the topic.

" You thanked me already but i couldn't let anything happen to you in my house my dad would have flipped"

I mentally noted that he only saved me cause he didn't want any troubles because of me so he still didn't care. Why did it even matter its not like we were friends anyway.

"So you decided to keep my clothes huh?"He said with a playful smile

"I really loved the shirt but i was to ask you when to return them to you but you didn't seem to be in a speaking mood."

"In that case keep the shirt but I'm coming for one of yours."

When one hour was over we left. He offered to drive me home but i told i was fine.

I walked home thinking about Blane he was so nice you'll think he was a different person. When i got home i went to talk to my mom. I got in her bedroom and saw her packing her bags and it didn't not look a two day trip.

"Honey we have to talk. "

CHAPTER 5: She left

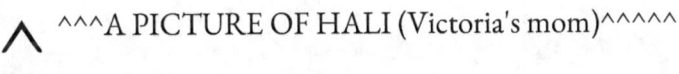 ^^^A PICTURE OF HALI (Victoria's mom)^^^^^

****

I sat on her bed cross legged as i waited for her to explain why exactly she was packing her clothes.

"So Honey I know you're probably wondering about the bags am packing.."

"No shit..."

"I have to go to Canada for a few weeks for work you know we really need the money.."

"How many week are we talking about?"

"Sixteen..."

"Four months... You are going to leave alone for four months?????"

I knew we needed the money but four months. Did she expect me to just live a lone for that long.

"Honey, You can't stay here alone cause i won't be able to pay for this place and the place i will be staying at.."

"So what Mom do we have some imaginary Relatives i don't know about?"

"No but yesterday when i went to met my friend she agreed to let you stay with her. She is really nice you will like her."

"But you said she is usually not around alot."

"I really don't have any other option Honey, please don't make this any harder than it has to be..."

Although she sounded sad i didn't feel it but she obviously was sad, she is my mom.

"Okay mom. I understand so when are you leaving?"

"Tonight, I called school and told them you won't be going to school tomorrow, Cici will be coming to help you pack and take you to ger place."

"What and you just told me about this don't you think you could have told me ooh i don't know yesterday or last week?"

I was mad this is the last i was going to see her for the next four months. But i chose to understand her situation and not make things harder for her.

She was already done parking and soon her Taxi was there to take her to the airport. I hugged her for what felt like an hour while a few tears escaped my eyes. She kissed my forehead and promised to call me ten times a day. Then she left.

I texted the guys about what happened and Iano and Ric came over cause they were the closest and it was already around 2 am. They came over with some Ice cream. They hugged me and we ate the tub of ice cream together.

"Tony"

"Hmm"

"Since your mom's gone we have the house to ourselves and i just mean me and you" Iano said and winked

I fake gagged "Iano never gonna happen even if I had to do it with you to save my own life"

Ric laughed. Iano looked at me with a smirk and told Iano to shut his hole. We continued watching TV while Ric kept on texting probably talking to Eva.

****

I woke up when i felt my phone vibrate it was 7 in the morning. I woke the boys up to go get dressed for school. They hugged me and told me to call them if i needed anything and they both kussed my forehead as they went to their house.

I went to the fridge which so basically empty and groaned as i felt my stomach rumbling. I heard the doorbell so i went to check on who it was.

When I opened the door i saw a blonde woman who looked like she was in her late twenties but from what my kom told me she was in her late thirties. I wanted to look that good in my thirties.

"Hello Victoria, I am Cici your mom's friend"

She seemed nice. " Hey Cici, come in..."

"I figured you'd need breakfast"

As if on que my stomach rumbled. "I was starting"

"Good thing i brought food" she said as she laughed.

As i ate her well packed breakfast she told me a little bit about herself. She was her husband's person assistant. She had to travel alot because her husband had alot of companies in many countries. When we were done we went to my bedroom and started parking. I kept some music surpassingly she sang along we even danced a little. I liked her already.

"Time to say goodbye to your house." She said.

Her driver came and helped put the suitcases in the boot. I looked back at my house for a few minutes before i looked up and got in her car.

The drive was nice Cici told me the driver could drive to school or i could drive myself since I did have my driver's license but i just didn't have the car. I really appreciated her hospitality. She even didn't seem to be bothered by my weight unlike everyone else i met. Which just made me like her more. The driver opened the door for us i didn't even realise we had arrived cause Cici was telling me about how my mom and her met it was hilarious.

"We are here"

I looked around to take in the environment. She lived in a mansion a very beautiful one. Something was familiar about it but i couldn't put my finger on it.

"So do you like my house?"

"Who wouldn't love all this" i said as i continued looking around.

"Hey beautiful" i turned around and saw a man approach Cici and give her kiss and asked her about how she was.

"Adam this is Victoria, Hali's daughter" Cici said to Adam.

"Hello Sir,"

"Hello Victoria, yoy can call me Adam"

I smiled and gave him a nod. He told me he had a son he was in school at the moment but i would get to meet him during dinner.

I was eager to meet his son. Considering his parents he would also probably be nice too. I was shown to my room. I couldn't believe that this room was going to be my room for the next four months it was beautiful. The bathroom was all white and very beautiful. I spent the rest of the time unpacking.

When i was done i talked to the boys and told them about the mansion that i was yet to explore. I told them about their son and they became all protective telling me if the boy bothered me i could just give them a call and they give him a talk.

I heard a knock on the door and Stacey the maid came in and told me dinner was ready and everybody was already at the table waiting on me. I put my pajama pants and a sweatshirt and went down.

When i got to the dining room i saw a face i knew all too well sitted on the table . When he lifted his head and his eyes met mine. I couldn't feel any emotion from him. I looked over to Cici and Adam.

"Am guessing you two know each other then.." Cici said feeling the obvious tension in the room.

"Won't you come sit down Victoria" he said. That was the first he ever used my first name to call me.

I slowly walked over to the table and Stacey served me the food she prepared and i mouthed a thank you to her.

CHAPTER 6: housemate

∧ ^^^^A PICTURE OF CICI^^^^^

Adam and Cici quickly finished eating and left the table, they said they had some work to finish up on.

"So you are they one that is going to be living with me?"

I just nodded as i mentally scolded myself for not realising the house that i almost drowned in. Or maybe it was because it looked a little different during the day. He chuckled and then looked at me. I raised my head and looked at him he didn't seem all that happy i was staying with him.

"Don't tell anyone your staying here or i promise i will make your stay here a living hell"

"You'd be embarrassed when people find out and we wouldn't want that would we?" I said sarcastically.

"We wouldn't, so don't go around bragging about living in a mansion for the next few weeks..."

I couldn't believe how much of a dick he was being. When i was done i said

"Ooh come now who would willingly tell people she is staying with the biggest Dick to ever walk the face of the earth!"

I got up and carried my plate to the kitchen. I would have helped Stacey clean up but i was honestly too pissed and she was almost done. So i just told her Goodnight and went to bed.

I kept thinking about how Blane was acting. I just kept my phone on silent and slept cause i had school the next day.

****

I phone vibrated waking me up it was six thirty. I went to the bathroom, brushed my teeth then took a shower. When i was done i wore my black trousers and a hoody. I had so many hoodies they were my daily outfit cause they hid my stomach and arms.

I went downstairs to the dining room for breakfast.

"Goodmorning " I said when i saw Adam and Cici having breakfast. It was already late so i couldn't sit down and have a proper breakfast. I took toast and Cici said she'd drive me to school. We were in the car when she said

" Adam and I will be going to London, you probably won't find us when you come back from school. So it would be just you and Blane"

I didn't even want to hear that frog's name.

"What about stacey?"

"Stacey is only there when Adam and i are around... Blane says he doesn't like having her around."

I was sad cause she really seemed nice and we kind of clicked.

"Its okay."

"I'll leave the car behind so that you can use it for going to school and other things"

I told her the car won't be necessary but she insisted she even left me a credit card if i needed anything for the house or wanted to treat myself to anything. She said she had no problems with money i could spend as much as i wanted.

"Do i leave the car here for you to come home with or.."

"No its no problem i will just ask my friends to drop me off."

"Okay take care, I'll leave the car in the parking lot at home the keys will be on your dresser"

I hugged her goodbye before she drove off. I saw my boys at their usual spot. I rushed to them cause i really missed them.

They got up and hugged me then kissed my hand. They asked me how i was and how i was adjusting. I told them about Blane but not the part about telling me not to te anyone about me staying there i told them not to tell anyone though.

We went to class and the day went by quickly.

***************We were in the Smoothie hut. We were laughing at Ric for being too loved up. I laughed at him but i wanted someone like Ric kind, considerate of others and someone who wouldn't hurt my feelings. I had never had a boyfriend. It didn't bother me cause i wanted to wait for the right one. Its not like boys were lining up to be my boyfriend but i pretended to not care.

"Hey Ian"

INSECURE AND CONFIDENT

I rolled my eyes wheni clearly recognised that attention seeking voice. I immediately excused myself and went to talk to one of the servers her name was Cynthia, she was beautiful but she didn't really put as much as Gwen in her appearance.

"now why would you leave Gwen and come over here and talk to little old me"

She was sarcastically as i rolled my eyes at the mention of her name.

"I just happen to prefer your company to that pawn of the devil"

She laughed and glanced at Iano. I knew she had a huge crush on him ever since she started working there.

"You know, you just stealing glances at him won't make him notice you...." I said to her. I saw a little blush on her cheeks.

" Ian notices people like Gwen not me"

"You haven't tried though.... I think he would like you if he knew you. How about this give me your number and i will invite you to hang out with us sometime."

I could see her face lit up but she tried to hide it. When she gave me her number and i saved it I saw the boys leave and head to the car. I then heard a honk.

"Okay that's me. Bye Cynthia"

"Bye Victoria"

I got in the car and we listened to hiphop and Brian tried to rap. We had to switch of the Radio cause he was a really bad rapper. I could see the mansion and i sighed as i got out the car. They told me to call them if I needed them to beat up someone.

"Bye boys"

I waved and went in. No one was in the house i was hoping I could see Stacey again but she was not around. I went to the living room to watch TV when i saw someone. I screamed then he woke up and had grabbed the vase that was close by.

"Hey relax, I'm Alex" he looked at me as if he expected me to know him. I raised my eyebrow waiting for him to continue.

"I'm Blane's friend"

I heard footsteps from the stairway I turned my gaze as i saw a handsome specimen come into view i suddenly lost my grip on the vase and it fell from my hands. I turned my gaze to the vase that was now broken because i couldn't get a grip on myself. I heard the boy chuckle and then he said

"Hey I'm Sam. Blane's best friend"

"Heeeeeeeerr....."

"You must be Victoria"

"How did you know?"

"Oh Blane told us you were uhm hard to miss uhm curvy" he smirked

I felt offended by what he said but i convinced myself the were obviously Blane's words.

"Okay.. "When i took a step i felt one of the glasses pierce my foot i let out a little sob. Who knew a small piece of glass would hurt that much.

Sam came towards me and sat me down on the couch and looked at my foot. He asked Alex to clean up the mess i made he was relactant but agreed. Sam took a first aid kit and removed the glass then cleaned my wound.

When he was done i thanked him. I sat down there for a while when i heard the door open.

"What are you doing?"

"I was watching TV, you that rectangular screen on the wall"

"Go to your room i want to hang out with my friends?"

I didn't even argue with him. He noticed the wincing i was doing as i walked but he didn't even ask about it. I got to my room and did my homework. Then watched my favourite series. Until i got hungry.

I decided to go to the kitchen and make something. When i sat down to eat Blane also came he had served the food and sat next to me. He didn't say a word and so did i. When he was done he got up leaving the plate.

"Blane" i called when he was at the door he turned around and looked at me without saying a word.

"You forgot your plate on the table.."

"Yeah so.."

"Its not going to take itself to the sink"

He looked at me for a minute before he turned around and said

"I'm sure you'll figure it out Martinez, Goodnight."

That man infuriated me. I got up and cleaned the dishes then went to my room and got some very much needed sleep.

CHAPTER 7: Broken windows

∧ ^^^^^^A PICTURE OF SAM^^^^^^^

****

The next few weeks were unbearable i even considered just crushing on Iano's bed but i thought of all the girls that probably had been there and i just chose not to.

Sam came over frequently and i always found an excuse to just lurk around and just stare at him. I was trying to be very subtle about it. But i think he noticed once or twice.

He asked me out. Sam freaking god looking Sam. We were having dinner nothing fancy just burgers. Blane obviously didn't agree, he was actually very pissed about it but he didn't say anything.

Cynthia was helping me get ready for my date. Yeah same Cynthia from the Smoothie hut. She was actually very awesome she hung out with us sometimes and the boys like her. Iano even flirted with her, but she told me she likes him but she also wanted something serious so until he's serious nothing was ever going to happen.

"Okay babe, I'm done with the make up"

I looked at myself it did make me prettier and it was very light make up it was hardly noticeable. She even made me go shopping she got me an off shoulder crop but it wasn't tight cause i was not comfortable and some ripped jeans.

"You know, without your hoodies on, you don't look that big.."

She was not wrong. I looked nice.

"I'll keep that in mind.... Thank you Cynthia really thanks"

I wanted her to end up with Iano and that's why he is the one picking me up alone so that he gets some alone time with her after they dropped me off.

Iano texted me telling me he was outside. I put on my shoes and we went downstairs. Blane was in the living room when he turned and looked at me. I stood there and looked at him. Cynthia went to the car so it was just us.

"You clean up good.."

"Uuh.. thanks"

I couldn't get my head wrapped around the idea of Blane giving me a compliment. He did seem to be genuine.

"So you and Sam huh?"

"Yeah he seems really nice"

"Pshht, whatever you say......... Just be careful okay... Don't do anything your uncomfortable with"

"Aaaw... Does the big bad Blane care about me" i said trying out my puppy eyes.

"You wish Martinez"

"Thanks though, I'll see you later"

I waved as i got out. I got in the car and kissed Iano's head and drove off.

When he dropped me off i got in and i saw Sam he was sat in a booth at the corner. He was looking like the meal i wanted to eat instead of the burgers and these were the best burgers in town and thats saying something.

I headed over to the booth and said hy as i slid in. I said hy and he asked about my day and all that stuff then we ordered our food. I wasn't exactly comfortable with him but who am i to complain.

We ate our burgers and had a little small talk. When we were done he paid for the meal even though i did insist on splitting it half way he refused.

We left the restaurant and we were in his car listening to some music. He suddenly turned it off and looked at me.

He leaned in on me and tried to kiss me i felt uncomfortable but it was Sam kissing me. I didn't break the kiss but i didn't reciprocate it. He moved in closer and held my waist. He tried sliding his hands up to my bra. And that's when i realized what he intended on doing. I pulled back but he came even closer so i pushed him off. He moved back looking angry.

"Okay Victoria your really starting to get on my nerves,"

I was confused what did i do he was the trying to pull down my bra.

"What do you mean your the one who is trying to touch me"

He laughed. He seriously laughed which made me a little bit confused.

"Okay what do want. I played your game i took you out. I even allowed as to be seen in public together. People probably thought we were on a date.."

When he said that i was ready to choke the life out of him and not in the wierd kinky way. But i kept my cool until he said

"So we aren't going to fuck?"

He asked as if he just asked me if i was not going to have ice cream.

"You fucking piece of shit...."

I got out of the car slamming the door he didn't even move. I needed to do something to get all this rage out. As if God heard my prayers i saw a baseball bat i picked it up and turned around to his car.

When i got to the back of his car dragging my new found weapon i stopped and took out my phone.

"Hey Blane, am in the parking lot next to the restaurant i was at come quickly before you have to help me get reed of a body."

That's all i said before i put on some music nothing emotional but it did suffice according to the situation. When the music was at its fullest volume i put my phone in between my boobs. And immediately smashed his car's back window. He got out of the car but i broke the right backseat window and he moved back. Right front window into pieces.

"What the hell are you crazy?"

"I think its best if don't speak unless you want this bat to be smashing something far more deserving"

When he moved closer i swang my bat and hit his arm. I couldn't care less. I went to his front window i smashed it but before i could finish up on the other two in the left Blane came rushing and that's when i stopped.

He looked at me. He wasn't mad. Maybe i was not stable and didn't see him well but it looked like admiration. He came closer and he directed me to his car and i followed.

I was in his car with my bat. We both left Sam on the ground.

When we got home Blane took me up to my room. He sat on the couch and just stared at me.

"I'm not going to cry"

"I didn't say you were"

"Then stop staring at me like that"

"Okay am going to my room just tell me if you need anything"

"I will and please just don't tell anyone about what happened"

"I don't think i have to, if people see it all over YouTube"

Of course someone took a video. That's all people seem to be able to do. He left and went to his room it was just across the hall. I went into bathroom to clean myself and remove the stench of the that monster from my body.

I was on my bed i couldn't sleep. I went to the fridge and took out a tub of ice cream and two spoons.

I knocked on Blane's room then i got in. He was in his boxers.

"Ice cream" i asked

He nodded and actioned me to go to him on his bed and i did. After a few minutes of laughing cause we were watching FRIENDS and who won't be able to laugh after that. He suddenly switched the tv off and turned to look at me. He looked at me as if he was feeling guilty then he asked me what happened and i told him what happened in the car.

"I'm really sorry about Sam i shouldn't have let you go out with him. Its not the first time he's done this. I should have known.I'm very sorry Victoria"

He looked so sad i felt a need to comfort him so i did i held him and pulled him in for a hug he didn't pull away.

"Thank you. i know he is your friend but please don't let him come over here while am still staying here"

"Of course he won't even come near you i promise"

****

CHAPTER 8: Not so rude Blane

∧ ^^^^^A PICTURE OF CYNTHIA^^^

****

The sun rays just couldn't let me sleep. I reaching for my phone to check what time it was when i felt someone's hands around my waste. Then i remembered everything that happened last night.

We fell asleep together. I was in his bed i was freaked out but it was very comfortable .

"Goodmorning Martinez"

That was not what i expected. I thought he was going to freak and tell me to get out but he didn't. He got up and headed for the door.

"Goodmorning Saint John"

He turned and chuckled.

"I like it, when you say it. Okay how about you take a bath and we can have breakfast together"

"Your being awfully nice I'll be right down"

He left his room and went to shower in my bathroom. I put on my hoody and a shorts. When i got to the kitchen i found Blane preparing breakfast.

"So you do know how to cook something"

"I never say i didn't know how to cook"

"Then why don't you....cook"

"Cause your here Martinez"

We sat down and had breakfast. I laughed alot. He was funny if he was trying to make forget about what happened it worked i completely forgot about it. When were done he took the plates and cleaned them.

"Hey Blane do you know where my phone is."

"I think you dropped it in my car let me get it for you"

He went to get my phone and brought it to me.

"Looks like many people saw the video"

He said before he handed me my phone. 97 missed calls 15 messages. I called Iano.

"Hello Iano"

"What the hell happened last night and why didn't you call me... You didn't even text me... Do you know how worried we all were... We had to find out through YouTube Victoria..."

He was shouting loud shouting. He was angry he is the one who called the most from the missed calls.

"Victoria are you even listening to me... I didn't even sleep last night cause i was freaking worried..."

"Am sorry I just dropped my phone in Blane's car i just got it but am fine now. Blane brought me home and I've forgotten about what happened. Please tell the guys am okay cause my phone is about to die. I'll see you in school tomorrow okay. I love you guys."

"We love you too take care Tony. I'll see you tomorrow"

I switched off my phone and charged it. Blane was at the pool so. He was swimming he was a good swimmer. I wasn't we all know that. He started doing what i think was backstrokes.

"Show off!!" I shouted at him

He stopped and came to the edge of the pool where i sat.

"Why don't you come in the pool"

"Okay and why don't go into a shark's mouth and see if you'll survive'

He laughed. I loved it when he laughed.

"I know you can't swim that's why i want to teach you. Every Sunday i will be your swimming instructor."

"I don't have a swimsuit"

"Remove your hoody and shorts. You can put on my shirt if you want."

I thought about it for a while but I did have to learn to swim to avoid what happened last time. I put his shirt on and got in the pool to shallow part.

"Come closer to me." He said and i moved closer.

He taught me the basics, i was still scared but i trusted him. We stayed in the pool for a long time it was almost four . When we got out of the pool.

"You now your very nice sometimes Saint John"

"And you can be badass sometimes Martinez"

We both laughed.

"You looked really sexy with a bat and messy hair looking all pyscho"

I blushed a little but i couldn't let him see that.

"You look sexy when your cooking in your boxers"

Okay i always knew i was confident but not this confident.

"Duely noted"

I switched on my phone. I got a text from Iano.

We want a sleepover ask pretty boy if its cool with him :) Iano

"Blane"

"What's up"

"My boys want to come for a sleepover and i might invite Cynthia too"

"Its cool can i invite my friends too"

"Yeah but not you know who"

"The whole world knows Martinez"

We laughed the video went viral labelled badass female.

Yeah he said it was cool i will also invite Cynthia and he is going to invite his friends too maybe two people ;) Tony

Okay no problem so Saturday is cool. Goodnight Tony :) Iano

Yeah perfect Goodnight Iano:) Tony

I was excited about Saturday. I was going to be Blane, Iano, Cynthia, Brian, Ric, Alex, Stacey and I.

I made dinner and Blane helped me clean up in the kitchen.

Then we both went to sleep. Cause the next day was Monday.

****

I decided to drive to school in Cici's car. It was one of these big cars and i got a few stares when i drove into the parking lot and got out. I ran to my boys i brought them in for a hug. I missed Frank bit his mother needed him in Germany and he traveled back two weeks ago.

I told to them what happened on Saturday and they got very mad but i told them i handled it they were actually very proud of me.

I didn't see Blane since last night he left early so i didn't see him but he made me toast. He wasn't in the classes we had together so i gathered he didn't come to school.

Lunch time. I got alot of stares and smiles. Stares i was used to but never smiles. I sat down at our usual table with my boys.

"So what do you guys think of Cynthia?"

"I think she's cool" Brian said

"She nice huh... What do think Iano?"

"Uh yeah yeah she okay why?"

"Hmm you know i called her to tell her about the sleepover but someone" i said looking at Iano "beat me to it"

"What i didn't do a bad thing did i?"

"Okay whatever,"

****

It was almost ten when Blane came home he was holding a bottle of alcohol. I went and sat on the couch and i sat next to him.we were both silent until he told who he had been.

"I went to Sam's house and told his parents about what he tried to do. He came out, he tried to beat me up so as we were fighting i hit with a piece of wood i saw and i think i hit him very badly he was rushed to the emergency room"

He looked like he was about to cry but he held it in

"I didn't mean to hurt him i just wanted him to get out if town."

I held him very closely to my chest where his head rested. He seemed to calm down. He pulled back and looked at me.

"You are very beautiful Victoria,"

No one ever told me that with the sincerity that i could see in his eyes. He leaned in as if he wanted to kiss me but he just took my hair and placed behind my ear then he got up and went to his room. After a few minutes of thinking about what happened i got up and went to sleep.

****

CHAPTER 9: Sleepover at Blane's

∧ ^^^^∧A PICTURE OF STACEY^^^^^^

****

During the week Blane and I didn't even talk apart from the normal wierd goodmornings. He was ignoring me but i couldn't understand why. Well it was Friday and i was pretty excited cause Cynthia and I agreed to have a pre sleepover. She would come on Friday and extend it to Saturday while the others are also there.

Rumours have been going around that Gwen, yes evil Gwen, had a boyfriend. I felt sorry who whoever had to deal with her ungrateful ass.

****

Lunch my boys and are talking about the sleepover they said they bring a few beers and it could be like a small party before the sleepover. I agreed seemed like a good idea.

When i lifted my head i saw Blane he usually sits with some boys from the football team but he was not alone.On his arm like an accessory was Gwen, freaking Witch, she saw me stare then she turned then put he hand around his neck and said that he loved him just loud enough so i could hear.

Since i have known Blane he had never had a girlfriend he would have just entertain a few.

I was angry like furious angry so i just got up and left before i did something i didn't want to. I didn't understand why i was so angry he was allowed to go out with anyone he wanted.

****

After school we went to the Smoothie hut and the boys left after a fee hours as i waited for Cynthia's shift to finished so that we headed home together.

We got home and ran to my room. That's when i decided to ask her about her and Iano.

"So on Saturday when i left you two alone what did you do?"

She blushed bright red it was hard to miss.

"He didn't take me directly to my place we went to the movies and had a good time like a very good time.... He was perfect at the end before he dropped me off he opened my door and then walked me to the door then he freaking kissed me but my dad came out... Wrong timing i know"

"Omg you guys kissed and you waited a whole week to tell me. That's why he called you and invited you before I could. I am very happy for the both of you at least someone's Saturday went well."

"I heard about what happened Vic am really sorry he is a dick but i heard he in the hospital guess Karma really is a bitch huh"

"If your referring to Karma aka Blane then yeah"

"Holy shit Blane beat him up for you"

"I guess you can say that"

"Well boys don't just go around beating up their best friends unless he likes you"

Well that was absurd Blane doesn't like me not even in his wildest dreams.

"C'mon Cynthia he is Blane Saint John. Tell me why exactly he would like me?"

"Well i guess we'll find out in time"

We watched some latest movies and talked about our future plans what we hoped for.

****

Saturday the day i was waiting for all week. Cynthia woke up very early while i slept in it was on a weekend and i did fancy my sleep. I woke up at nine amd was just seated on the couch texting and laughing.

"Who are you texting and why do you so happy?"

"No one. Now go shower i will go make breakfast"

I didn't argue I had just woken up. I took a shower and put on Blane's T-shirt and a pair of shorts that showed of my ass. Before I went downstairs i called my mom and we talked for while she told me she was having fun and it made me feel better about her not being with me.

Breakfast was good. We sat and waited for the boys. Cynthia decided to go for a swim and i just watched her as i cheered.

The boys came at around four with beers not alot though but enough. Alex and Blane were here too. We just talking about random stuff. The door opened it was Stacey i had not seen her since. I got up and hugged her.

"I see someone missed me"

"I did alot how have you been."

"Good. I missed you too"

"Who wouldn't"

We all laughed then she said hy to everyone else. Time had passed and the guys were a little bit drank so we decided on a little truth or dare.

"Truth or dare Victoria" Alex said

"Dare"

"Bold choice.... Okay i dare you to make out with Blane"

"What! No freaking way he has a girlfriend remember"

"I don't mind" Blane said

"Okay three minutes Am timing you guys you stop when i say stop" Alex added.

Blane and i stood up and came toward me and stopped when there was barely space between us. My whole body wanted to do this but i couldn't allow myself to do it. Just when we were about to touch lips we heard the door bell.

"I'll get it" i said as i ran to the door.

When i opened the door i wanted to slam it back closed.

"You've got to be kidding me.... What do you want Gwen?"

"I came to see my boyfriend its his house last time i checked"

She walked past me and went to the living room where everyone was. I followed behind her. No one seemed happy to see her not even Blane. He went to Blane and sat beside him.

I got so angry at how close she was to him.

"Alex!"

"Start that freaking timer"

"Yes ma'am"

I went over to Blane and pulled him towards me and we made out Infront of Gwen. My blood was boiling but when i heard Alex say stop i did and went straight to my room.

We had sleeping arrangements cause the house had extra rooms. It was Iano and Cynthia , Alex was to be in Blane's room so now he had to share with Brian. Stacey decided to sleep in my room and Ric had his own room. Yeah the house had six rooms the master bedroom was for Cici and her husband.

Stacey came in followed by Cynthia.

"Hey sweetie" Stacey said

"Hey Stac, Hey Cynthia"

"So am thinking Blane's girlfriend wasn't invited"

"Ya think.... I have no problem with her as Blane's girlfriend if that's what your thinking, she just bullies me alot in school that's why i don't understand why Blane would go out with her"

The sat on my bed and pulled in for a hug.

We went back downstairs and i wanted to talk to Iano so i called him to the kitchen.

"Hey Sweet cheeks" i laughed at that pet name

"Hey Iano" i was seated on the island and he came closer to me he stood in the middle of my thighs and i hugged him.

I let my head rest on his shoulders and it honesty felt better but i moved him away before Cynthia got the wrong Idea.

"You've changed Tony"

"Changed how"

"Changed as in bolder... First the sam dude.... Then kissing Blane Infront of Gwen.... Your becoming badass.."

That word really started rubbing up on me. I liked it.

"I just react without thinking when I'm mad."

"Damn, Well i want to be there every time you get mad"

We laughed them headed back to the living room. Blane went up to his room but he asked Gwen to leave. But he wanted to be alone. Which meant Alex was in Brian's room. Not that they complained.

*****************I woke up next to Stac, she was beautiful she would probably be Ric's perfect match but he was with Eva. I got up took a shower and made breakfast for everyone.

I went to Blane's room. I found everything messed up his books were all over the floor his lamp was broken his knuckles were all bruised. I took a first aid kit and i cleaned his wounds. I was putting on his bandage when he woke up.

"What are you doing in my room?"

"I came to wake you up for break....."

"Get out"

CHAPTER 10: Accidents

∧ ^^^^^A PICTURE OF ALEX^^^^^^^^

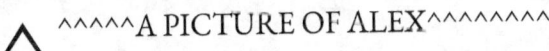

****

Blane was angry with me but i didn't understand why. When he asked me to leave i did. We all had breakfast when the boys came down. Cynthia and Stac helped me cleaned up. When we were done were all by the pool watching the boys swim.

"Hey Cynthia"

"Yes Vic"

"How did you sleep yesterday?" I asked wriggling my eyebrows so that she knew exactly what i was talking about.

"Well....... Nothing happened between Ian and I but we talked for about 3 hours didn't sleep much"

"Huh he must like you....... He didn't try anything with you?"

"He didn't. Although at some point i did want him to "

We laughed " Okay..... I'll be right back" I got up and went in the house everyone else was outside. I had gone in for redbull. When i saw Blane he was carrying a bag. I was hesitant on asking him about it but I did.

"Where are you going Blane?"

"Out. I'll be staying at Alex's place for a few days"

"Why...... Did i do something wrong?"

He just looked at me. I thought about asking him if it was about the kiss. Just the thought of that kiss made my lips tingle.

"Are you leaving because of the kiss yesterday?"

He chuckled. " Bye. You can ask Stacey to stay with you."

He went to his car leaving me confused amd very angry. I took my keys and took Cici's car. I followed him. I know i can do really stupid stuff when I'm mad but its who i am. He stopped at some hotel. I waited a few minutes and before I got in.

I went to the receptionist and told her i wanted to hand him his phone he had forgotten it in my car. She was hesitant at first but agreed eventually.

When i got to his room i saw him he was looking at the view from his window.

"Blane"

He turned around quickly obviously not expecting to see me.

"What are you doing here Victoria? Did you follow me?"

"I followed you........you were angry"

"So Victoria..... What if I'm angry how does it concern you?"

"Why are you angry?"

He moved closer to where i was standing until i had raise my head to maintain eye contact.

"I am angry because of you."

"I'm sorry I know i shouldn't have kissed you Infront of your girlfriend....."

"I thought you and Ian were just friends?"

"We are just friends"

"Okay look Victoria just get out."

"Why are you asking about Ian?"

"Because i saw you two making out in my kitchen yesterday."

"We didn't make out he was..."

"Look Victoria am not interested in some excuse just get out don't come back here"

"But nothing happe...."

"Get out Victoria" he shouted and pushed the vase that was nearby and it broke just a few steps from us.

I turned around and got out. Who was he to judge me. I was angry more than angry i was furious. I took my time to check on him and thats how he treats me. He tells me to get out of his hotel room. Even if i did make out with Ian why would it bother him. I didn't make out with Ian he just stood in the middle of my legs as we hugged.

I was too distracted by my thoughts when a car was just about to hit mine when i turned i tried to avoid the car i hit a tree and that's all i could remember before I blacked out.

****

Blane's Pov

We were standing so close to eachother all i wanted to do was feel her lips on mine again.

"Get out Victoria"

I was angry at her. When Gwen came to my house. I didn't invite her. I didn't even like her she was supposed to be a distraction not my girlfriend even Victoria thought she was. She wasn't and i did make that very clear before i asked her to leave after Victoria kissed me.

I never wanted the kiss to end but it did. She went to her room and the other two girls went to talk her.

She came back down and called Ian. I wanted to apologize to her for Gwen but when i got to the kitchen he was between her thighs. His head was on her neck. I felt hurt i couldn't control myself i wanted to take my anger out on Ian. I went to my room and i broke anything that was breakable. I threw my books all over the place. Before i fell asleep.

I felt someone's hands on mine but i liked how it felt. I slowly opened my eyes for a moment i was happy to see her next to me. Until i saw my room that was not beyond recognition. I asked her to get out of my room.

I couldn't see her face and not see Ian sucking on her neck. Even the thought of it made me angrier. I decided it would be best to leave for a few days to cool down.

When i was about to get out i heard her voice asking me why i was leaving.

"Out. I'll be staying at Alex's place for a few days"

I wasn't going to Alex's place because i wanted to be alone. So i was going to a hotel. She asked if i was mad about the kiss. I wasn't, i loved our kiss.

"Bye. You can ask Stacey to stay with you."

After i said that i got out and just drove to the farthest hotel from house. I got to the hotel checked in.

She followed me to the hotel. I just wanted her to leave me alone. I wanted to get her out of my head. I aksed her about what i saw. She said nothing happened that they were just hugging. My heart believed her but my brains told me to react on what i saw. I asked her to leave.

She looked angry. She had the look she had when Sam tried something with her. It made me worried about her. I cursed myself for caring so much. I got out and followed her. She was driving very fast.

It almost as if her hands were on the wheel and directing the car but that's it. I was honking when i was a car coming right towards her.she turned her car trying to avoid the car but instead she hit the tree.

I got out of my car and called an ambulance as i tried calling out her name if she could hear me. The ambulance arrived and they put her on the bed and put her in the ambulance.

"Are you a relative?" One if the men asked me.

"I'm her boyfriend" i said quickly without thinking Incase they didn't allow me to go with her.

I got in the back of the ambulance with her and drove to the hospital.

When we got to the hospital they took her into the emergency room but i wasn't allowed in. I called Alex and told him what happened and he said they'd there soon.

Few tears escaped my eyes. I blamed myself for what happened to Victoria. If she didn't recover i didn't know what i would do.

CHAPTER 11: After Accidents

I felt a sharp pain in my head. When i tried to open my eyes. The room was bright, very bright i had to adjust my eyes.

I looked around i saw tubes connected to my hand . I looked around I saw Iano on the chair.

"Ia...."My throat was very dry but he heard my voice nad woke up he passed me a glass of water.

"Hey Tony, how are you feeling?"

He looked like he hadn't slept in a while. He had bags under his eyes his hair was messed up.

"Pain... That's how I'm feeling... How long have you been here?"

"Since Sunday... Its Tuesday"

It wasn't serious i just hit my head on the steering wheel. The doctors said i was very lucky to have had such minor injuries. After the doctors did their check ups i asked if i could go home and they said it wasn't a problem.

"Where's everyone?"

"I actually wanted to talk to you about something?"

"Yeah you know you can tell me anything"

"Okay then uh I wanted to say that the reason I refused to leave you alone is because uhm"

"Cause you looowvvee me "

He laughed awkwardly.

"Yeah love about that...."

"Hey Victoria" Blane walked in.

I was happy to see him. I had been waiting to see him since i woke up. He didn't look like himself he looked like he hadn't taken care of himself since Sunday.

"Hey Blane... You don't look so good?"

"Your one to talk"

I laughed at least he was being friendly.

"Okay will both you get out now so that i can get changed and go home."

They got out and i changed. Blane brought me a pair of trousers and his t-shirt the one i loved. I smiled when i saw it then rolled my eyes.

When i was ready i got out and they drove me home in Blane's car.

When we got home everyone was their even Alex. They all hugged me and i could see the relief in their eyes.

"Aaaaaaawww......Y'all making me feel really special maaan"

"Thats cause you are Martinez"Blane said

I couldn't help but blush a little i guess some of the guys noticed.

"Okay I am hungry who else is?"

"Actually we were just leaving. We just had to see you and make sure you were on your feet again" Cynthia said.

They all left it was just Blane and I left.We walked into the kitchen and Blane pulled out a chair for me to sit in.

"Okay Martinez you can have a seat and you watch me looking sexy while I cook"

I laughed cause he remembered when i told him he looked sexy when he cooks.

"With pleasure Saint John"

He winked at me before he started cutting up the ingredients. I later remember I had to call my mom cause Ian told her about the accident. She was relieved when she heard my voice, she even wanted to come back home but i told her she didn't have to. When i was done talking to her the food was ready he even served me the food.

I loved it when blane was all nice and caring. I also liked it when he was rude it made him more appealing. I know i am wierd but i just made me want to pin him to a walk and violate him i ways he didn't think possible.

"Victoria I'm really sorry for shouting at you and telling you to leave this wouldn't have happened if i didn't get so mad over something really stupid"

"It's okay Blane its totally my fault I can be unstable at times. I know you were angry cause you thought Iano was kissing me but why?"

"I don't know but I made you a gift to show you how sorry I am but that i will show you after we are done eating"

I was intrigued he even got me a gift. He must have felt really bad. We finished our meal and he took the plates to the kitchen and i helped clean them.

He took me to my room then he placed his hands over my eyes so that i Couldn't see. He opened the door and led me in. When he removed his hands from my eyes. I saw a baseball bat framed in a case and placed on the bare wall beside my bed.

"OMG Blane you've gotta be kidding me"

"You don't like it"

"What in the world would make you think that "

I was happy. I was ecstatic. It was the same bat i beat Sam with and broke.his windows. That bat was a symbol of how badass i could be and i needed the reminder once in a while.

"If you don't like it i could..."

I turned around and grabbed him and pulled him closer to me. I kissed him. He was hesitant at first but he kissed me back. The kiss was passionate you'd think we were soulmate. I could literally her the fireworks. He wrapped his hand around my waist and pulled me closer to him. I didn't want it to end but we had to pull away for air. Then i looked at him.

I remembered Gwen. I know thee worst timing but i couldn't help it he had a girlfriend.

I had just kissed him fully aware he had a girlfriend. I didn't do that cause it was wrong. I got out i ran out to the pool.

I looked up at the sky and all i wanted to do was go back and finish what i started.

He came outside where i sat. And also looked at the stars.

"Do you think its true what they say about angels watching over us?"He asked

"Yeah i think its true"

"So my mom's probably looking at me right?"

I was confused. I got up and looked at him waiting for an explanation to what he just said. He got up and looked at me too. He looked as if he was going to cry in the next minute. All i could think about was consoling him he looked sad.

I remembered the tape i saw on the day of his party. I have never gone into the room since I went to live there. The woman was unconscious and Adam took the baby that she was holding.

That was Blane's mom. She died after delivering her baby. I didn't want to aske Blane so that he could prove whether or not my theory was right. But i couldn't. He would open up if he wanted to.

I just held him for a while and we just stayed in that position for a while.

"Wanna swim?"

He looked me the way a dog would look at a bone.

"As long as i get to be on your back while you show off"

"Challenge accepted Martinez"

"So confident Saint John"

"Its part of my many charms"

"Okay dumbass"

He got into the water with his boxers. He looked beautiful in the water while the moon reflected on the water. I couldn't help but stare.

"My body is also one of my many charms"

"Egotistic fool"

He held his chest as if i just hurt his feelings . I took off my trousers and got in.

"Okay hop on Martinez"

"Aye aye Captain"

He turned around amd i got on his back. I wasn't that heavy cause we were in the water so i didn't care. I wouldn't let him carry me while we were on land. I didn't want to responsible for his broken bones. He swam impressively well then i got off his back. We splashed water at eachother for a few minutes then decided we should go back inside.

We went in then i changed and when i was in my towel i went to his room. I opened the door and got in he was in the bathroom.

I opened his closest and took out a shirt. Everything was arranged back to its place. And the broked things were replaced. When i was about to go to my room he came out in his boxers.

Did i emphasis on how amazing he looked in just his boxers. He was just supposed to be a work of art. He should have been on display so that the whole world could appreciate God's creation.

"This staring contest your having with my body is making my ego grow by aloot"

"Yeah yeah Blane "

"C'mere put on the stolen shirt and sleep with me."

"What "

" I sleep better with you next to me "

"Aaah why not"

I went into his bathroom and put on the shirt and got out. I got into bed next to him when i was comfortable he pulled me to him and but his head on my shoulder.

"Goodnight Martinez"

"Goodnight Saint John"

CHAPTER 12: Old Memories

I woke up alone in Blane's bed. I knew he wasn't at school cause he said he would stay home with me and take care me. I was fine but i wouldn't pass up a chance of him being all nice and sweet.

I took a shower and went to the kitchen for breakfast. Blane had already prepared breakfast ans was waiting for me.

"I almost thought you would sleep till the afternoon"

"Goodmorning to you too Saint John"

He came closer to me and held my head. He planted a kiss on my forehead and said "Goodmorning Martinez"

I felt my heart beating. I wasn't used to him being all sweet. But it felt warm and welcoming. Almost alluring.

We sat down and talked for a while as we ate. I told him thank you for the yesterday. He did take care of me. Ian called me today morning and asked me about how i was.

We were in the sitting room watching tv. I took the remote and reduce the volume.

"Blane can i ask you a personal question and please don't mad"

"I was wondering when you'll me about my mom?"

"How did you know that"

"I could see how curious you were yesterday but i do i appreciate you not asking me about it then"

"It's okay I just want to know better and i was really surprised but please don't feel obliged to tell me"

"Get up follow me"

I was hesitant at first. But i got up and followed him. He took me to the home theater room. He ushered me inside and told me to sit down.

He played the tape from when he told me to get out. But he played it from the start. It showed Blane being placed in his mother's hands. She held him and smiled and said his name. But after she did she passed out. The

Adam his dad was standing next to them when he screamed at the nurse to take the baby away as he held his wife. The doctor rushed and checked on his mother. He signed and shock his head. His mother was dead. Adam was crying he even sat on the floor. He got up and came closer to the camera i presume he was talking to the person holding the camera he said that he did not want anything to do with the cursed child. He had taken what he had treasured most in the world. Before he finished talking the video was over.

Blane's eyes were dry. I could see how hurt he was. He looked as if he hated himself for what happened to his mother. Almost as if he also blamed himself like his father did.

"Blane I am so sorry for what happened to your mom but it wasn't your fault"

"How can you say that Victoria. Even my own father said it was my fault."

"I don't think your mother would want you to feel this way "

"At least now you know why he and Cici are not around alot"

"So Cici is your step mom"

"Technically she is my aunt, she is my mom's sister, they had the same name, Cecelia, but it was too confusing hence Cici. She took care of me even tried to make dad stay home more but he refused he said he couldn't handle seeing me for longer than two days"

"I don't know about your Dad Blane but i know that your mom doesn't blame you for her death neither should you "

"Thanks Victoria, i was alone for a long time just had different nannies every 2 months so that i won't het too attached to any of them but i found Sam and Alex they became my family and i am very sorry for what he did to you but he was not that bad as a friend"

" I still hate Sam but i am happy that he was there for you when you needed someone"

"He was. I told you all this so that you would can understand me better and we could know more about eachother. It also why i am sometimes uhm difficult"

I laughed so did he. "I guess i understand"

I pulled him in for a hug and we stayed like that for about ten minutes then i thought about opening up to him you know cause we were sharing and all.

"Since we're opening up "

"You don't have to tell me about anything you don't want to Martinez"

"But i want to so shut up and listen"

"You are so bossy... I'm listening"

"Logan Martinez also known as my father... When i was small i was uhm chubby obviously, it bothered him but my mom told him it was just my childhoodness or whatever and that the fat would reduce as i grew older but it didn't so when i was five i heard him and my mom argue he said that i wasn't his child since i was fat and he wasn't. He told my mom that he was leaving he wasn't going to raise someone else's fat kid." I sighed. I could feel the tears wanting to fall from my eyes i only told my boys this story but that was long ago.

"You don't have to tell me Victoria"

"No i really want to please let me do this"

"Okay"

"He left that night i saw him through my window with his bags he didn't even bother to tell me he was leaving. I got out and ran to my mom's room she was on the side of her bed crying her eyes out and i just went to her and hugged her she hugged me back. I asked her later on why dad had left she said that they had problems between them and that it had nothing to do with me. I knew she was lying but I didn't want to her to know i knew cause maybe what she told would be better to believe than the fact that he left because I was fat."

"Victoria i never knew about that. He doesn't deserve even the honour of being your father not even in paper cause you Martinez are the strong person i have ever met. You can be kind and compassionate. You don't let anybody bring you down and that Victoria i why i fucking Adore the shit out of you "

I laughed cause no one had ever said that to me.

"Back atcha the strong part the kind part definitely not you"

We both laughed.

"come on i'm not that bad."

My head was on his chest. I turned and looked at him. He looked at me then came in closer to my face. There was nothing i wanted more than to devour his lips but i turned my head just in time.

"Blane you have a girlfriend"

"Okay Gwen, not my freaking girlfriend I'm really getting tired of everyone thinking she is."

"So she is not your girlfriend"

"Yes Martinez. She and I nada"

"Nada" i said as i raised my eyebrow

"Nada Martinez, so can i kiss you know"

"Don't ask me stupid questions and kiss me already"

I said and he did just that. He kissed the shit out of me and i loved it.

CHAPTER 13: No longer Secrets

All was right in the world. Well in my world it was. That week was one of the best i had in a long time except the accident part.

The next week was also undeniably better. We had breakfast together i prepared that but Blane insisted he would prepare dinners for both of us. He really was a good cook. Secret talent maybe.

I still went to the after school smoothies with my boys and they were coming over tonight it was all Brian's idea and we agreed. Blane was also cool with it he also invited Alex. Stac was not around and Cynthia said she was really busy with something.

****

The boys were already there we all watching television.

"Ric how's Eva and when the hell are we meeting her"

"She's cool. You will you just have to be patient. I don't want you guys to meet her till I'm sure she the one."

"Hmm okay Ricky"

"And you Brian any new people in your life?"

He was nervous. He looked uncomfortable with the question. He looked around and cleared his throat then looked at Alex and he gave him a reassuring nod.

"I wanted to tell you guys something"

"Yes Brian what's up?"

Everyone's attention was on him even Iano put down his phone.

"I am Homosexual"

He looked at his fingers not lifting his head.

"We are kind of dating" Alex said.

We were all surprised but Blane was emotionless.

"I didn't tell you guys earlier cause i felt like y'all would look at me different"

I got up and went to comfort one of my bestfriend's

"I am sorry Brian if we ever made you feel like you couldn't be open to us about your sexuality and no one sees you any differently okay we all love you... You too Alex"

"Thanks you guys, i love you guys too."

Everyone came in for a hug even Alex. Blane got up and went upstairs i had him bang his door.

"Welcome to the family Alex, break his heart i break you understand" i said while i held his collar.

"Yes Victoria geeezz..... I wish Blane understood"

"I'll be right back lemme go talk to him"

I got up and gave him a reassuring smile. I left Iano congratulating Brian and Alex for finding each other.

I opened Blane's door he was just on his bed looking up.

"You have a wierd was of reacting to good news Saint John"

"Its not am not happy for them.... I am but"

"Well Alex thinks other wise.. what's the problem"

"Alex and I..... he is the only family i have left since Sam left. He only had me like i only had him.... But now he will also have Brian... Do understand what i am trying to say"

"I think i do. And you Blane don't only have Alex. You have me too. I will always be here when you need me as i am sure Alex will too"

He got up and looked at me. I loved how he looked at me. It was as if he could only see me no one else. And it just tingles through my whoke body.

"I guess your right i do have you. And Alex will always be there for me"

"I know I'm always right"

We went back downstairs and he talked to Alex they even hugged it out. The boys had a few drinks and when we were all tired we went upstairs. They insisted on sleeping in my room except Blane he still wasn't very comfortable with Iano, Ric and Brian.

I was on the bed with me and the others were around me. Just as used to sleep in my room in my house. I felt like nothing changed.

****

Sunday morning had become my favourite part of most weeks. Blane kept on giving me swimming lessons.

I was becoming attached to Blane and i wasn't sure if it was a good thing or a bad thing but it did feel right. I liked Blane.

I woke up and Blane was already waiting for me in the pool i was in his t-shirt. The boys were still asleep and i didn't want to wake them up yet.

"Almost thought you would miss your morning swim classes"

"Goodmorning to you too Saint John. And no I wouldn't miss these classes for a meeting with the president."

"Good to know you enjoy our Sunday mornings and we need to get you a swim suit"

"Yes i do. And No i really love the one i have already"

I was able to stay afloat so i wouldn't drown just incase but i couldn't hold my breath for that long. We were working on the swimming part then.

"Thanks by the way for the lessons"

He was now holding me close to him our faces were close to eachother.

"Anytime Martinez"

Me moved in and looked at my lips the whole time. He kissed me i kissed him back obviously. This kiss was different it felt like he wanted more than just a kiss.I gave access for him to deepen the kiss and he did.

"Really Victoria you haven't even known this guy for five minutes and your already.... Uuhrg God"

Ian he saw us. He had already stormed off. I felt guilty very guilty like I cheated on him or something. I moved away from Blane and got out of the pool.

"Fuck Ian wait"

He was in the parking lot when i got to him. He was angry but i didn't understand why. I didn't tell him about Blane and all the kissing but i didn't do anything wrong did i.

"What's wrong Ian it was just a kiss its not like we are having babies!!"

"Really Victoria. Why him of all people."

" What's wrong with Blane?"

" Your so clueless"

"Clueless about what Ian"

He just stood there. He laughed mockingly and then scoffed. He looked hurt i had never seen him this angry at me. Was it so wrong kissing Blane. He made it seem like i had broken a law or something.

He didn't react this way when I kissed Blane the last time during the sleepover.

"You really want to know why I am so angry ."

"Yes Ian. Why exactly are you angry?"

"Because Victoria i tried to tell you at the hospital but he showed up and ruined the whole thing"

"Yeah i remember then he Blane walked in "

"I wanted to tell you to confess cause i had finally gotten the courage to tell you. When i heard about the accident i was a mess Victoria that's why i decided i would tell you finally open up about what i have trying to show you for so long"

What did he want to tell me. He wasn't getting to the point and it curiosity was eating me up.

" I love you not love in a friendly way i am in love you for as long as i could remember. I freaking love you Victoria"

CHAPTER 14: Oblivious Victoria

I didn't know what to tell him. So i just stood there and remembered when we were fifteen and i was telling him about how all the girls had boyfriends and i hadn't even had my first kiss.

He kissed me. Yes Ian was my first kiss and i was his but he told that after the kiss. He told me "One day Martinez i will also be your first boyfriend"

I thought he said that because he didn't want me to feel bad. I thought he was just giving me comfort i even scoffed when he said it.

But there he was Infront of me confessing his love for me but all i could think about was Blane. Why was I thinking about him when one of the people who would never hurt me even in my dreams said he loved me.

He was still standing there waiting for an answer. I looked back and saw Blane he was standing there as if he was also waiting for my response which I didn't have.

I looked at Ian who i had known my whole life. And i said tried to form words but what came out of my mouth was stutters do i just turned around and ran till i was in my room.

All the boys had woken up so i was alone in my room. I couldn't believe how clueless i had been. I couldn't remember a moment when Ian wasn't the one who would be there to help me or just make me laugh.

I loved Ian. But i wasn't in love with Ian. I considered him an elder brother. I would do anything for Ian even learn to be in love with him but my heart had its own ideas.

****

I stayed in my room but i had a snack stash so i didn't get hungry. The sun was already setting so i decided it was time to get up and head downstairs.

I was in a sweatshirt and my short shorts. I went into the living room, Blane was watching TV then he turned to me with a smile.

" I thought you'd stay in there till tomorrow"

"I didn't want you to miss me too much"

"Yeah right, everyone's gone its just us"

I sighed in relief i really didn't want to see how disappointed Ian looked.

He got up and went into the kitchen. He came back with a tub of Ice cream.

"Ice cream makes everything better"He said

"Thanks"

We eat the ice cream together and avoided the topic. It was getting really late so we decided to got to upstairs.

I went to his room and i slept in his bed cause he asked me too. Not because I wanted to be close to him and look at him sleep. Lie.

****************I got out of the car. I saw my boys on their usual spot. I took deep breaths and went to them. But when Ian saw me i smiled at him but he got up amd left. I said hy to Brian and Ric.

Classes were boring amd i kept on thinking about Ian he didn't even speak to me. I was determined to speak to him during lunch.

Lunch he was nowhere to be seen. Even Ric didn't know where he was. I figured I could talk to Ric when we went to the smoothie hut. Brian was not joining us cause he had to be there for Alex when he came out to his parents.

It was just Ric and I. Cynthia came in for her shift i waved but she completely ignored me. I brushed it off and decided i will talk to her as soon as i was done talking to Ric.

I asked him if he knew about Ian's feelings for me.

"We all knew Tony, even Frank. We talked to him and told him to talk to you about it but he said it wasn't the right time yet. Ypu really are clueless huh!"

They all knew, But i was oblivious after all the things he did for me.

"Uh Ric i Really had no idea. How's he doing? He has been avoiding me"

" He's good he just not himself. He mainly just stays quiet ams doesn't want to talk about it"

"Ric you know i love your brother but i love him the same way i love you and Brian and Frank. You guys are like my brothers. I don't think I will be able to be in love with Ian"

"It's okay Tony. Love isn't forced just talk to him. It will take him some time but he will heal."

"Thanks Ric. I hope we could go back to normal i would hate myself if Ian and I kept on not talking"

He sighed. "So Blane huh?"

"Don't start..." He laughed "Okay I have to go see you tomorrow"

He got up and left. I sat there and went through my phone for a while. I saw Cynthia without customers so i headed over to her.

I said hy to her but she didn't even spare me a glance. I honestly didn't know why she was also angry at me. So i asked her severally what was up with her until she told me.

"Want to know 'what's wrong'.." she did use quotation marks with her fingers before she continued.

"You know what i freaking knew Ian you. I wasn't blind i could see how he looked you when you didn't notice. But you told me to go after him if i really liked him and i did. I was stupid enough to listen to you and I put myself out there and now I just feel stupid all because of you"

She had snaped. Even Cynthia noticed that Ian had feelings for me. She hadn't even known him that long .

"I'm sorry Cynthia. I had no idea Ian had feelings for me. I'm really sorry if i made you feel stupid."

I got up and went to my car and drove off. I drove till home.

Blane wasn't home. I was bumbed cause he was the only I could think of that could distracte me from all the Ian drama.

I took the opportunity to call Cici and say hy since we hadn't talked in a while. We talked for a while before I decided to also call my mom.

I video called her cause I had really missed her and her face I also wanted to ask her about the Ian situation to get her advice.

After i explained the situation.

"Sweetheart we both know what you should do. You've known him for a long time and I know you don't want to loose him. Call me and meet up. Talk to him he needs exposure and then maybe his feelings for you would no longer be a problem. I know you'll do the right thing.Amd P.S even i knew he liked you"

"Wow so everyone knew except stupid oblivious Victoria Martinez "

We laughed and i suddenly heard a voice.

"Honey food's ...."

I knew that voice all too well. It was a voice i wished i would never have to hear. He was silent once he saw me on the screen amd my mom was shocked terrified even. The face i grew to hate day by day but never faded from my mind.

What was hse doing with him. I was furious i disconnected the call. My phone kept on ringing it was her again and again. I so angry i threw it to the wall and felt a little bit relieved when i saw the phone break and lay on the ground.

I shouted. I screamed. For what felt like hours until Blane came home. He came to my room in a hurry but he didn't ask why i was having another one of my wierd break downs.

He just held me as i balled my eyes out. He didn't say a word. My head rested on his chest as he hugged the rest of my body and moved me clser to him. I felt my anger reduce to a normal level. We just stayed there but didn't say anything.

CHAPTER 15: Happy State

The rest of the week went by with just glimpses of Ian.

My mother kept calling me non-stop i even shut down my phone cause it got irritating.

Blane didn't ask me about my break down not that i wasn't planning to tell him but i just didn't get the right time.

There i was in Blane's arms. His arms had become the only thing that could comfort me. We were on the couch watching friends and laughing our asses off and i wouldn't change it for the world.

I was thinking alot about Ian and i was planning on talking to him, so i texted him.

I miss you Ian, smoothies maybe? X Tony :)

I got up and turned to Blane.

"My mom Left me here to go to shack up with Logan Martinez. She didn't tell me i accidentally found out the other day"

"Ooh your dad that's why you had your uhm.."

"If you are trying to say break downs then yes. I just don't understand why she would lie or even want to see that man again"

"Maybe it isn't it what you think Martinez"

"What else could it be a harmless get together for old times sake"

"Yes maybe,"

"Come on even you don't believe that.."

My phone vibrated then i checked. Ian replied.

Hey Tony meet me there in 20. X Ian :)

"I have to go meet Ian.... I gotta go"

"Just you and Ian"

"Yeah why you jeeealous"

"Yeah right" he rolled his eyes "bye Martinez"

I could see it he was jealous. But at that moment i had to leave and go meet Ian. So i put on my trousers and went to my car and left.

When i got there he was on our booth waiting for me. He didn't look himself he looked disturbed. I went to him. I asked him how he was and he said good. We talked a little about how he was doing trying to avoid the inevitable but avoid it for long.

"So about what you said on Sunday"

"Bet you were surprised huh"

"Its not everyday someone is told says they love me"

"Guess feelings not mutual"

"Uuh Ian i love you, so much i probably do just about anything for you but i always say as a brother and suddenly you say you loved me."

"I didn't mean to drop it on you like it's urgh You kissing Blane it felt like my heart was being ripped out and i couldn't do anything about it"

"I'm really sorry about me and Blane i thought you guys were asleep"

"So you and Blane are like together or"

"Oh no no no no. We just make out once in a while"

" Really Victoria so just go around kissing guys"

"No Tony he's using you. So tell me this do you like him?"

"I don't know Ian maybe I do can please drop it "

He scoffs and co concentrates on his smoothie. We talked normally with about how his week had been but i kept thinking about what he asked me did i really like Blane?

I talked to Blane and told him about my mother and her ex husband. He was angry about me not telling him immediately it happened cause he knows how much it hurt when i was younger when he left.

"It doesn't matter we are talking or not, i am mad at you or not you tell me whenever something bothers you okay Tony. Cause no matter how angry i might be i always be there for you Victoria. Never doubt that."

"I really do love you Iano"

We got up and hugged it out. It was getting late so i had to get back home. I told him bye and left.

When i got in i looked for Blane. He was in the kitchen with a well prepared dinner for two. He even laid put the plates and everything.

"Is all this for me?"

"Don't flatter yourself I just got bored"

"Yeah whatever floats your boat Blane"

We ate and he asked about meeting with Ian. I told him we made up an we are still friends. Then he asked me if he said anything about him. I stiffened a little when i recalled Ian asking me if i liked Blane.

"He thinks your just using me"

He kept quiet for a while i could the anger from his facials.

"What do you think? "

I just shrugged. Then he asked.

"Do want to go on a date uh with me?"

He sounded unsure of himself. I was shocked. I had even stopped eating. For a moment i allowed myself to believe he liked me.

"Victoria?"

"Oh yeah.....yes of course I'll go on a date with you Saint John"

I was excited beyond excited. But i couldn't help but wonder for how long would my happy state last for. He said would go the next day.

After the food..i helped Blane clean up and we went to his room to watch a movie. I slept before the movie even got halfway through.

****

Author's note

Well this chapter was short..... And this is my first author's note. Hello few readers. I would really love reading your thoughts on the book so far please comment and tell me what your little heads are thinking of my book.

Mbbyyeeee

CHAPTER 16: All good until

A PICTURE OF VICTORIA'S OUTFIT

*************************I woke to Blane's beautiful face being hit by sun rays which made the sight all the more alluring.

"Its not polite to stare Martinez"

He said. I thought he was asleep. I woke up a little bit embarrassed.

" I wasn't staring"

"So you weren't thinking about how gorgeous i am looking"

Was he reading my thoughts or something cause that's exactly what i waa thinking but i couldn't let him know that.

"You wish"

I headed to my room to wash up i put on my just biggest sweatshirt. I do admit i was thinking about our date later on i was ecstatic. I went to the kitchen to appease my stomach. When i got the kitchen he had already made breakfast a very well laid out variety of morning foods i might add.

" Trying to be charming Saint John"

" Some things I am naturally good at. And besides what better to kick off our date"

"I thought that was later"

"Yes the whole day just me and you on multiple dates this is the first come."

I sat down and devoured the different foods. He really out did himself the food was delicious. When we done eating i wanted to clean up but he refused he told someone else would do it just for that day.

"Go change into something comfortable I'll and meet me in my car in 15 minutes."

"What my XXXL sweatshirt doesn't make make you want to devour me"

He laughed. Cause we all know no one would want to have to have sex with mw after seeing me in this thing but i loved it nevertheless. I went to my room and put on a jumpsuit and a top underneath that showed my cleavage but it didn't bother me and a pair of converse. I went to the car and he was waiting for me.

"Perfect" he said.

I couldn't help but blush a little. I got in the car he was staring at me but it felt good him looking at me like that like he liked what he saw.

"It's not polite to stare Saint John" i said

He chuckled a little then we drove off. I had no idea where we headed but i did like surprises so i didn't ask.

A familiar song was blasting on the radio. Just the way you are by Bruno Mars. I sang along and the next songs were also familiar soon enough we were singing at the top of our voices. I liked Blane's voice he could make it as a singer.

"You have a beautiful voice you know"

"Yeah it's one of my secret talents that's why I took up piano lessons"

"That explains the piano in the house. I wonder what other secret talents you possess"

"I can let you experience another one tonight if your up for it."

I laughed. He was referring to his abilities in bed. I had no doubt he would be good but why not tease him a little.

"Oh I'm sure by the time your breathless three minutes won't be over"

"Is that i challenge Martinez?"

"Take it as you will Saint John"

The ride went silent as we listened to music. I took out my phone and went to the group chat of me and the boys to check on them. Everyone was good so i switched off my phone and soon enough the car came to a stop.

I was like a small forest I don't know how to put it but it was nature at its finest.

"I will haunt you if you kill me and bury me here"

"Relax don't you trust me"

"Meeeh"

He told me to follow him into a the small forest it looked like a pathway. I followed him then he stopped at looked up so did i. I was beautiful. It was a tree house but a very well built one it had lights and everything it was simply magnificent. I just stayed there and admired it for a while when Blane cleared his throat making me turn my attention towards him.

"Cici bought me this piece of land and I designed this tree house for myself she paid for everything, my dad has no Idea of course"

"Its very beautiful Blane thanks for bringing me here"

"Your welcome let's go in "

We climbed the stairs and the interior was just as beautiful he had bin bag chair and a huge TV set. I went to the balkon to look around i could see a small playground five minutes away.

"Is the playground also yours"

"Yeah call me childish but those swings and slides are fun."

"Can we Go have this fun you speak of"

He laughed and then agrees so we head to the playground. The closer i was i could see it was built in a way that also adults could play and have fun.

Ww first went on the slides we played there for a while t until he started to chase me around the swing set. We laughed alot he caught me many times no surprise there. I sat on the swing for a while then i challenged him. Who ever could get at the highest point gets to tell whatever they want to the other person and the must do it.

He won. He decided it would be hilarious to see me dye my hair pink. I agreed since I'm the one who challenged him.

We went back to the tree house but we didn't go up. He led me behind the tree it was covered with a blanket the pulled it down revealing two chairs comfortable ones you could stretch them out for your legs. There was a projector that was faced towards another blanket. There was also a kind of roof so that the sun could penetrate just a little. I loved it.

"Second portion of the date"

" I love it Blane"

He motioned for me to sit so i did. We watched Sixteen candles cringy i know but i do recall telling him i had never watched it.

It was getting late. We had to leave. I loved the tree house it was so separated form humanity it made me feel free.

On the way back i was thinking over the days events. I wouldn't change anything that happened. We pulled up at a restaurant. It wasn't fancy or anything. Teenagers came here alot for burgers fries all the fast food stuff.

"I thought we were going home"

"What kind of gentleman would i be if i took you home on an empty stomach"

"I wouldn't use the word gentleman but whatever"

He laughed a little then we went in. Teens were there but not that many. We sat i was facing the door so i could see anyone who walked. When i saw a group of boys from my school and Gwen and he puppies i excused myself to go to the bathroom.

I stayed in the bathroom for a few minutes before i decided i won't let a bunch of stupid teenagers ruin one of the best days I've had. When i was about to go out i saw them stand around Blane.

"So whatcha doing with Fatty Vic" one of them said and the all laughed. "Don't tell us you have thing for fat people" another one added.

I stayed were i was as i they kept on adding their thoughts. Their thoughts didn't bother me i was used to them but the fact that Blane just laughed together with them instead of standing up for me. It broke my heart. When i was about shed a tear i heard Gwen add "Even her dad didn't want her who would"

I was mad. I was very insecure about the reason my dad left and here she was saying it like it was nothing. I couldn't just stay hidden and listen i heard enough.

I got out of hiding and went to where they were. They couldn't see me going towards. When i got to where they were i pulled Gwen's hand so that she could turn and face me and immediately i saw her face i slapped her.

"See Gwen what your not gonna do is air out your opinions about my personal life cause you have no fucking right to do so. It's not like giving my opinion about your dad beats up ypur mom. So please put my personal affairs out of your mouth. Understand!"

I didn't even want to hear her response i turned and just left the restaurant. When I was outside walking away i heard him call my name. I honestly wasn't in the mood to face. He sat there and listened to them as they insulted me. He called out again and again.

"What do want Blane can't you get the hint!"

"I'm sorry Victoria..."

"What are you sorry for saying we are just friends or was is it for listening to them insult me or maybe it is because your ashamed of me cause I'm just the fat girl from school who is leaving at your mansion huh"

"No Victoria just listen to me"

"No Blane just leave me the fuck alone."

I continued walking away i had tears in my eyes. I was stupid to believe that Blane Saint John actually like me. He always ignored me in school for goodness sake me always avoided me in school. How could I not see it earlier he was embarrassed by me. I took my phone and switched it on and called Ian to pick me up.

He want close to where i was so i didn't have to walk alot. When he picked me up he just drove me to his place cause i didn't want to see Blane's face then. When i got to his place i just drifted off to sleep.

CHAPTER 17: Spa

I woke up with puffy eyes. I groaned at how i looked. I took a shower and went downstairs. I only saw Ric and Ian's mom in the kitchen. I said hy and she told me the boys went to school, they thought i should have a drama free day. They were right all i needed was just a day to relax.

I loved their mom she was like my second mom. She always took care of me when my mom came home late or whenever i stayed at their place.

She told me she had asked if would agree to a girls day out i agreed. She really was good company.

*****

We had a fun day at the spa. She insisted that i needed to professional touch or whatever. We were a restaurant having a late lunch.

"So Victoria wanna tell me what's wrong?"

"I was kinda hoping you wouldn't ask"

"How could I not when i can clearly see your not okay"

I told everything that has been going on from my mom and Logan to Ian telling me about his feelings and the fantastic day i had with Blane that got ruined at the end.

"Uh Victoria that's alot but i think you should try and hear your mom out I know she loves you she always has."

"I guess i could pick up one of her calls"

"Good. And i knew Ian had feelings for you"

"Ooh no not you too everyone knew except me"

"Yeah. But that only means that you are not in love with him which is not bad and I'm glad my son understood and you guys are still friends."

"I am too."

"Now this Blane kid. I think he likes you but not enough to stand up for you. Do you like him"

"Yes Blair i really did like him now i just don't know"

"If he does like you he'll try and make right. So promise me you will give him another chance"

"Argh why Blair he is the one who messed up and I don't want to through yesterday's experience again"

"Promise me Victoria"

"Uuh I promise okay"

We went back home and talked about for a while before Iano and Ric came back home. Ric came and gave me a hug then when he went to freshen up Ian came closer and held my face in his arms.

"How are you Tony" Ian asked

"I'm good thanks for yesterday"

"Anytime. Wanna watch a movie"

"Sure"

We went to his room and watched a comedy movie while me made fun of the characters. When the movie was over we just sat on his bed and talked. Then there was silence when Ian decided to speak.

"I know you said you are not in love me but I am in love you Tony and I'm not asking you to magically fall in love with me I'm just saying don't fall for someone who doesn't deserve you "

"Thanks Iano. I'll keep that in mind"

We got back to our jokes. He even told me about how people were talking about how i stood up to Gwen.

I had to go to school the next day. Saying i was not excited was an understatement. We went downstairs for dinner. After the amazing food Blair made i helped her clean up and went to sleep.

****

I woke up and took a shower. When i was in a towel Blair gave me i realized i had no clothes all my school stuff was at Blaine's place. I groaned and called ian at the top of my lungs.

"You don't have to shout geez"

"Ooh sorry thought you were still asleep"

"Well if i was that would have definitely woken me up so what's up"

"Uhm i just realized I had not clothes and my school stuff was at Blaine's place"

"Yeah i realized yesterday that's why i went by his place and picked up some stuff they are in the car lemme get them"

I sighed in relief. I really didn't wanted to miss any more classes. Ian came back with all the things i needed. I thanked him and he said he was waiting downstairs. I quickly got dressed and went down.

I got in the back Ian was driving Ric was seated at the back texting.

"Talking to Eva"

I said as i turned to face him while wriggling my brows. He rolled his eyes. We pulled up in the school's parking lot. I saw Brian immediately coming towards me. I smiled i really missed him. When he got to me he hugged me tightly.

"I missed you" he said

"I missed you too since you and Alex started going out i rarely see you"

"I'm sorry i wasn't here for you"

"Its okay"

He pulled away and smiled he was cute when he smiled Alex really was lucky. I still remember on his first day he came to me and he said he wanted to be my best friend but i already had Ian and Ric so he just settled for being apart of our little family.

We headed to class i quickly caught up on what i had missed the day before and the day went on smoothly except this thought that kept bugging me at the back of my mind, Blane.

Lunch time in the cafeteria. We were in our usual seat when i saw him walking in alone he didn't even take any food he just walked straight to where i was. I watched him as he came closer and closer and finally got to me.

"Can we talk" he said.

I just looked at him so were the boys i could see how angry Ian was.

"You don't want to wait till we are home alone your popular friends might see you talking to me"

"Would you stop with the bullshit Victoria"

"Bullshit I'm the one with the bullshit. Your the one who is full of bullshit matter of fact your a coward! A fucking coward!"

I picked up my bag and left while i saw the little crowd that had formed start to keep on moving. I was angry he is the one who is wrong. He is the one who couldn't fucking defend me and I'm the one with bullshit.

I kept walking till i was in the parking lot. I had no idea where i was going cause i didn't have the car here.

"Fuck" i shouted.

I felt a hand on my shoulder try to calm me i immediately knew it was Ian cause i saw me follow me. I turned around and hugged him as i tried to calm myself. He hugged me tightly.

I pulled away and we just stayed for a minute while i looked at his eyes he did have the most beautiful eyes they were so soft and alluring. I could his eyes shift to my lips. I looked at his too. He leaned in and we so close i could feel him breath.

"Victoria"

That's when i snapped out of my trans it was Blane. I moved away from Ian but Blane had already left. I was just about to kiss Ian. I turned around and left. I had to leave i could hear him call out to me but i just needed time to think about what i was i about to do.

CHAPTER 18: Carnivals

I really needed to go around with my own car. I always end up needing a ride but i wanted to be alone so i just called an uber. There was a carnival in the neighboring city it really wasn't far and i desperately needed a distraction. Good thing i always carry cash incase of emergencies.

I arrived at the carnival, my mom used to bring me here when i was feeling down it wasn't always open but somehow always was when we needed the distraction.

I walked around heading to my favourite place. I had two places i loved the first place was the sea horses for children i loved watching kids having a care free time their laughter was infectious.

The second place is the rollercoaster seeing people scream and while some threw up was just hilarious. But i have never been on a rollercoaster and I'm not planning to.

As i sat at a point where i could hear and see people scream laughing at the top of my lungs they start to hurt when i decided i had enough.

I walked around and saw a guy selling cotton candy and why not.

I went to the guy and when he stopped twirling it to give it to me he i gave him a very mean look. Any adult would be insulted by the amount he was about to give me.

"Keep going buddy" i said and he got back to it.

"Either your really pissed or you seriously love cotton candy" he said

"Both" i said blankly

He pated the seat next to him and i happily obliged. Yes i was willing to talk to a complete stranger about my problems.

"Here you can devour your cotton candy while i listen to you vent"

"You would seriously let a complete stranger blabber about their problems to you"

"Believe it or not selling cotton candy isn't that interesting."

We both laughed and i chose to talk to him whats the worst that could happen. He listened to me. And i found out his name is Coda, cute name he was attractive himself.

"So any advice Coda"

"Hmm well Victoria if you gave me your number i just might offer you some advice"

"Trying to flirt with me Coda when i just told you about two guy problems I'm having"

He chuckled a little "No Victoria i wouldn't put myself in a position like that i really like you but you seem cool and when I'm having problems you have to repay the favour by listening to me"

We both laughed. I think the sugar got me overly energetic.

I took out my phone and gave him my number. He said he'll text me so i didn't take his.

"I think you should talk to this Blane guy and find out what you guys are so you can stop wasting your time if he is not serious with you"

"Your right but I'm scared Coda."

"Why are you scared?"

"Rejection Coda what if he was just playing with me cause i was available, what if he doesn't like me"

"Listen Victoria, i have i known for two hours and I like you what's not to like. But if he does reject you, you take it and you get over it like the strong person you obviously are it will be his loss"

"I don't know if its your words or the sugar but i want to confront him now"

"Definitely my words" he winked.

He was packing up cause it was getting late. We walked to the parking lot and he offered me a ride home. I told him it was a little bit far but he insisted.

When we got to Blane's house i invited him in but he said he had to be somewhere maybe next time.

I walked in the house after taking deep breaths i was ready to confront him. He wasn't in the living room so i went to his bedroom.

I opened the door somehow wishing he wasn't home but he was on his bed he wasn't asleep we was just looking at the roof and i didn't fail to notice the empty tub of ice-cream on the floor.

"Blane" i said a bit unsure.

He didn't reply so i went in and stood Infront of him. I called him again then he got up and stared at me.

"Let's talk"

"Wanna talk Martinez okay let's talk"

I took a deep breath and sat next to him i didn't know how to start so i stayed silent i wanted him to start. Then he did.

"Why would do that?" He asked. He looked hurt.

I was silent. Cause i don't know why i was about to kiss Ian. I knew that was what he was talking about but i had no reason.

"Fucking answer me Victoria why were you almost about to kiss Ian?"

"I don't know alright. Maybe because he was there for me, maybe because i know he won't hurt me and will fucking stand up for me when a group of low life teenagers talk about me to his face."

We were both mad. Our voices were raised.

"I'm a coward Victoria is that what you want me to say cause i am I know i am. I should have defended you Infront of those guys and i didn't "

"Why didn't you Blane? why didn't you stand up for me?"

"Its not that i didn't want to Vic i just"... He growled " i just wanted to protect my reputation in school I know its stupid"

"No Blane it's not stupid its completely selfish what do you think i would have done if someone said horrible things about you. I would freaking defend you why because I'm a decent human being who doesn't care about what people think"

"I know that now. Look Victoria i know what i did was wrong and i should have defended you. It was selfish but I'm sorry ""Why did you even bother taking me on that date if you knew it would ruin your reputation. Why kiss me? why even talk to me or even ask me to sleep on your bed with you.? Why do all these things. Call me stupid Blane but i actually thought you liked me and maybe i read all that wrong but you misled me with the whole date thing. If you did it on purpose Blane your are an even more selfish bastard than i thought"

"I wasn't misleading you Victoria, I've just been in denial for a long time"

"I don't understand you Blane"

He moved closer to me were so close i cloud hear him breath and just immediately he smashed his lips of mine. Maybe it was his way of rejecting me. Call me stupid but if that was going to be out last kiss i was going to make it worth it.

I kissed him back and he licked my lip asking for access which i gladly allowed and he slipped his tongue in my mouth. Everything was in synch you would say we were perfect together. He both pulled away for air but he had my bottom between in teeth before he let go of it.

"I like you Martinez"

CHAPTER 19: Not just friends

Either i was intoxicated from all the sugar or i just heard Blane Saint Freaking John say he liked me. I pulled him in and smashed my lips on his. He kissed me back but i slipped my tongue in his mouth this time. Then we pulled away gasping for air.

"Either I'm hearing things or you just said you liked me"

"Mhmm you just want me to say it again"

"Will you? Just to be sure"

"Victoria Martinez, i Really really like you even before you came to live with me. I don't care what people think as long as i have you. Yesterday was hell i couldn't sleep just cause you were angry with me. And P.S i think your sexy"

"Wanna get some ice cream?"

He laughed "Really i tell you i like and you want ice cream"

"What i know you want some too"

"Lets get ice cream then Babe"

I felt the butterflies in my stomach flutter everywhere. We went downstairs his hands wrapped around my waist but i didn't bother me one bit.

I pulled out the tub and we went to the living room. After finishing another tub of ice cream we went to my room cause his was a mess.

******"***

I heard my alarm ring and i Just wanted to throw it to the wall but i had to wake up. I turned around and was faced my a very handsome face especially with the sun rays on his face. I took my phone out and took a picture of him and i was proud to say i just woke up next to one of the most attractive men i know.

"Done admiring me?" He said with a very sexy morning voice with a smirk on his face.

"Don't flatter yourself"

"So didn't just take a picture of me?" He asked as he raise his brow facing me.

"Ugh your a pain in the butt" i groaned as i woke up and went to the bathroom locking the door so that he didn't get amy ideas.

I did my daily routine and i felt a little brave so i decided to show some skin. I put on some ripped jeans and a black long sleeve blouse that showed off just a little bit of cleavage with was perfect.

I went downstairs he was already dressed he even prepared breakfast.

We sat down, eat and soon we driving off to school in his car he insisted. We got to school but when i was about to walk away from him he pulled me back. He held my hand and walked with me i couldn't help the stares i was getting.

When i saw my boys i told him i had to go he was resisted at first but gave in bit he kissed my forehead and told me to keep away grom Ian but i just rolled my eyes.

"Jealous are we?" I asked lifting my brow at him he shrugged and took me phone he did something then returned it to me.

"See you later babe"

"Yeah yeah" i walked away from him and went to the boys.

I said hy to all of them but Ian seemed off i knew I had to talk to him later. I made small talk with Brian about his love life until the bell for class rung.

The classes went on smoothly and we had a test the next week on Friday i had a reminder for me to study already set.

Lunch was normal Blane and I kept stealing glances at one another cause we couldn't seat at the same table.

"So Tony you and Rich boy are official or he's still fooling around with you?"

Ian asked in a rude tone i might add. I rolled my eyes.

"I wouldn't say official but he's not fooling me "

"Do suddenly you trust him Victoria, have you forgotten what he did to you God how can be so stupid"

"Watch your mouth! I'm not stupid and yes I do trust him and don't you dare call me stupid"

Brain and Ric were silent and Ian was really getting on my nerves.

"Fine do whatever you want Victoria but when he finally bangs you and leaves you don't come crying"

He got up and left before i could say anything. I hated fighting with Ian but he had to accept Blane i know he's not the best guy in the world but the heart wants what the heart wants.

When school was finally over i went over to Blane's car and he was there already waiting. I got in and he gave me a quick kiss as we drove off.

He didn't go straight to the house we went shopping first.

When i was picking up some stuff i saw these two girls looking at me and then at Blane. I was getting uncomfortable when they approached me when Blane went to get something.

"Hey your friend is so handsome do you think we could maybe get his number?" One of the girls told me.

was i jealous of cause i was. Was i angry or freaking cause they called me his friend. I mean we are not officialor anything but I'm definitely not his friend.

Before I could even give her an answer I felt a hand wrap around my waist and i immediately felt the tingles i always get.

"I'm her boyfriend and no you cannot have my number" he said in an annoyed voice.

The girls left and went away feeling embarrassed i could see it by how fast they walked from the situation.

"See how gorgeous i am every female wants to get some of this" he said looking at himself.

"God! how much cockier can you get"

"Come on babe you know its true"

"Btw I'm not your girlfriend"

"Do you wanna be?"

"Ask me then we'll find out"

He smirked and i thought he was going to ask me but he didn't. Instead he asked me if we needed bread.

I heard my phone vibrate and i at my phone when i noticed something i didn't before.

My wallpaper it the picture I took of him when he was asleep or thought he was. He put himself as my wallpaper. I wasn't going to change it cause that picture was freaking adorable and sexy at the same time.

I got a text from an unknown number.

Guess who? :)

I hated it when someone did this but i knew who it was.

I don't know is it the pizza guy:)

I'm offended no more cotton candy for you:)

What's up Coda. Miss me already:)

"Who are you texting smiling like that"

"You know Saint John for someone with your ego you sure do get jealous alot"

"I just like having your full attention is that so bad"

I rolled my eyes when phone vibrated again.

How about coffee on me on Saturday you owe me :)

If didn't know any better i would say you just wanna see me but okay Saturday 11:00 :)

Its a date :)

Don't get it confused you might get disappointed. Goodnight Coda :)

Can't a man dream without them being shuttered. Goodnight Victoria :)

I put my phone in my pocket and looked at Blane he was arranging the stuff we bought in its right places and was watching his muscles flex and i was enjoying every single moment.

We watched a movie and soon enough we were all cuddled up and drifting off to sleep.

CHAPTER 20: Parents

The rest of the week went on great. I woke up at 9:00 I wanted to sleep in more since it was on a Saturday but i had to meet Coda.

I got up a took a shower when i came out Blane was already awake. He got up when he saw me.

"Goodmorning Martinez"

"Goodmorning Saint John"

He kissed my forehead and asked if i had plans.

"Yeah i have to meet my friend, Coda i told you remember"

"Oh yeah sure I can't come with"

"I'm pretty sure he just wants to speak to me"

"I'm going to have to meet him if he the reason you didn't sleep till 11 on a Saturday"

"Are your trying to say I'm lazy"

"I didn't but you just did"

"Fuck you"

"If that's what you want"

I gasped and threw him a pillow.

"Pervert!"

He got out and went to the pool for a swim. When i was done i went downstairs and told Blane bye and drove off.

I arrived at the Café after about it was about an hour away from Blane's house. When i got there Coda was already waiting for me.

I said hello to Coda and ordered Coffee and a box of donuts for both of us of course.

I observed him for a while he look like he was in desperate need of sleep. He had bags. Even his hair was unkept and he looked like he just put on the First thing he say.

"What's wrong you don't look so great?"

"Just family issues,"

"You can tell me if you want"

He took a minute as if thinking about my offer then he said

"Its a long story..."

"I'm hear to listen to you aren't I.. Believe it or not speaking to Strangers helps alot"

He chuckled a little.

"I wouldn't say your a stranger"

"Good now I'm all ears"

"My dad, he and my mom are not very good terms he left over two months ago saying he needed a break. I know they have being having problems but i thought they would get through but i don't see that happening. It happened once when i was little they kept on fighting but the figured it but i don't think that's the case this time. My mom is drinking and doing drugs she almost over drugged herself earlier this week"

"Coda, I'm sorry your going through this but I think you guys would be better off without him if he is causing all this pain"

"That's what i think but my mom is so in love with him she just……"

He held he nose rubbing it.

I got up and hugged it felt like a natural thing. He accepted my attempt to comfort him.

"I don't know why Victoria but talking to you is just really refreshing"

"I'm hear for you anytime"

I went back to sit and gave him a smile. I thought of how some men could just be such bastards. How could he have such a wonderful family and leave them for some other woman.

After a few minutes he decided to loosen up a bit so we just talk a little bit and he said he had to leave. He insisted on paying for the coffee and donuts so I let him.

"See you soon Victoria"

"You too Coda"

I got in my car while he got in his and we headed in totally different directions. I got to the house, the house had grown on me and i had less than a month before my mom comes back. I would miss sleeping in the same bed as Blane though. Helping him study cause he really needed to get his grades up. His grades were good but he could do better.

When i got in i just wanted wanted to go straight to bed. That's before i heard Cici's voice.

"Hey Victoria. How are you, i missed you so much"

"Hey Cici I'm good. I missed you too"

I know we didn't interact a lot but i liked her she seemed nice. And she did take care of Blane like her own son.

"When are you guys leaving?"

I turned around and saw Blane leaning on the door to the kitchen.

"Ooh come here my sweet boy i know you missed me"

Cici went over to Blane and hugged her he smiled at her and hugged her back.

"I did miss you but i would have preferred it if you came alone"

"You know this is still my house boy"

I turned to see a pissed Mr. Saint John glaring at Blane. I could literally feel the tension radiating from them. Blane rolled his eyes and turned back to face Cici.

"We'll catch up later, Victoria and i have somewhere we have to be...." He turned to me " Victoria, I'll meet you in the car in 5 minutes."And he left and went outside.

I just went upstairs but when i got there i totally forgot what i came for and when i came downstairs i over heard Mr. Saint John speaking

"See how rude that Boy is he didn't even greet his father."

"Well do you blame him it's not like you act like his father"

"I already take care of all his expenses what more could he want a pat on the back or should kiss his forehead everyday before he sleeps...."

He went silent when he saw me standing on the stairway. He cleared his throat and went into the leaving room.

"Have fun Victoria we'll catch up tomorrow"

"Okay Cici"

I left and went to the car and got in. Blane was just looking at the road when he was driving he didn't even say a word to me. I decided not to speak cause he would probably not answer me.

We drove and drove and i got very curious. I asked him about where we were heading bit he said it was a surprise so i didn't even bother to ask again cause he wouldn't tell me.

We came to a stop it was on a hill to. I looked beautiful cause the sun was setting. He told me to get out of the car and we sat down on a blanket he brought . We cuddled as we watched the sun go down it really was romantic. Like movie shit romantic.

"You know Blane i didn't picture you as the cheesy kind of guy"

"Guess i have many sides you don't know... Yet"

When the sun was completely down he turned to face me. He said he had something for me he went to the car and he came out a little velvet box. He came closer and opened it.

He told me to close my eyes and i did reluctantly. He pushed my hair from my back and placed a necklace on my neck. Then he said i could open my eyes.

It was the most beautiful necklace i had ever seen. It was probably the most expensive thing i had placed on my neck.

"Blane I can't...."

"You can please don't refuse the necklace i saw it and thought of you please please don't say no"

"But Blane i never owned something so expensive"

"It wasn't trust me"

"Uh Blane don't lie to me"

"I'm not and i lost the reciept so I can't return... Just accept it"

"Well.... Thank you Blane but you shouldn't have and don't buy me anything this expensive again. Don't buy me anything period."

"But you look so beautiful"

"Thanks Blane"

I hugged him for a while and pulled back. We just sitting staring at eachother. When he took out his phone and then i heard my phone beep so i took it out. I saw five pictures send from Blane i looked at him suspiciously.

I opened the pictures.

The First one was him holding a paper written WILL.

In the second picture the paper was written YOU.

In the third picture the paper was written BE.

In the forth picture the paper was written MY.

In the fifth picture the paper was written GIRLFRIEND.

"WILL YOU BE MY GIRLFRIEND." He said.

CHAPTER 21: Strawberries

I looked at the pictures again and did i mention how stunning he looked in these pictures. He was shirt-less making funny faces except the last picture he looked like he was trying out the puppy dog eyes he was just so adorable.

I couldn't help it. I knew it was stupid but the tears just let themselves out without my consent. I looked at Blane. I not that i was thinking about my answer it was pretty obvious but i just realized i was falling in love with him.

I admit i was scared but I won't deny myself this glimpse of happiness.

"Yes Blane. I will be your girlfriend so from now on you don't refer to me as Victoria i am Baby, Queen, Babygirl, Princess and which ever name you so desire" i looked at him he was just stared at me.

We suddenly both burst into laughter. I didn't know what that was about i just came out. I always something I've wanted to say but i never thought i actually would.

"Okay girlfriend and from now on you may refer to me as Daddy or Papi or love of my life and which ever name you so desire"

I laughed again he joined in. I cringed at the thought of calling him Daddy but maybe he wasn't serious.

After talking for a while i got cold i was getting really dark.

"C'mere"

I moved closer to him and he held me it was like he was shielding from the cold.

We talked for a while and just enjoyed each other's company.

"We should go" he said.

So i got up and when i was about to head to the car door he pulled me back. I landed on his chest, his strong chest, i held his chest and he held my waist he then leaned in and kissed me.

I kissed him back. It was different this time it was as if he was trying to savour the moment. Like that moment was the most the most important thing on his mind.

We finally pulled away and i looked at him and he smiled. It was perfect until he decided to Open his mouth and ruin it.

"I can't wait to do that Infront of Ian" he chuckled.

"Don't you dare!.... I still need to talk to him don't go near him"

"Argh your no fun"

I rolled my eyes and we got in the car and drove back home.

It was quiet so Cici and Adam were already asleep. That was good cause i really didn't want their negative energy to ruin the moment.

"Blane can i talk to you"

I mentally scolded myself for speaking too soon. Blane turned to me and told me to wait for him in his room he wouldn't take long then he kissed my forehead and went to his dad.

I hoped they wouldn't have a big fight. I went to his room took a shower and i was on the bed i tried to wait for him but my eyes couldn't stay open any longer so i let my eyes close but not before i texted Blane Goodnight hopefully he would see it.

****

It was bright outside when i opened my eyes i looked at the time it was 11. It was almost afternoon. Blane was not in bed with me so i thought maybe he was in the bathroom.

I called out his name but he didn't reply. I sat up on the bed and stretched myself when the door suddenly opened.

It was Blane holding a tray of food.

"Goodmorning Baby " i smiled like a little girl on Christmas morning. I looked at Blane, he was my Christmas gift.

"Goodmorning " i said wriggling my eyebrows.

He laughed as he came closer and kissed my temple. And placed the tray of food Infront of me.

The tray contained bacon which i loved, a boiled egg since i didn't like when its cooked and strawberries which were obviously not mine since i hated strawberries but the orange slices were mine. There also was a cup of tea.

I was happy. I looked at him like he was the most important person in my life. We ate. Well i ate he just had the strawberries.

After the breakfast i went to shower up and put some clothes on. Blane told me Cici wanted to talk to me. And he had to leave and meet Alex. I really didn't want him to leave me but I let him.

I went downstairs and spotted Cici watching some reality show that i didn't really recognise.

"Hey Cici"

He turned and said hello then she asked me to join her and i happily agreed. She asked about school and how my stay was in her house. She even asked me about my accident i didn't know she knew about that Then she mentioned my mom.

"Sweetie, Your mom has been through alot you have to hear her out ."

"I know and i will I just don't want to see her with him. Huuh" i let out a sigh nad she nodded in understanding.

Adam, called her and she excused herself. I took the chance to call my mom cause i really missed her.

She picked up on the first ring. He looked okay i just smiled and she smiled back.

"How are you doing mom?"

"Better now that you called me.... I'm really sorry honey i didn't tell you about your father being here with me"

"Please don't refer to him as my father..... and it okay we'll talk about it when you come home and I don't have to see him"

"Uuhh Honey, i need to tell you something..." I nodded for her to continue "I am going to be coming back but i won't be alone"

"Your bringing him back here to our house. HE LEFT US MOM DON'T YOU GET THAT"

"I do Honey but...."

I didn't let her finish i hang up the phone. What was wrong with her.

He was the one who decided to leave us not the other way around and now he can just waltz back in like he just went for a freaking vacation. No, why Cause it didn't work like that.

If you walk away you don't get to come back. and that was it.

I got up and went to Blane's room. I really needed him i wanted a hug anything but i didn't want to interrupt.

The person i wanted to call was Ian but i need to give him some space so i called Ric.

I told what happened and he said he would pick me up which I agreed i really needed the distraction.

I also told him about Blane and I's relationship. He was happy for me. Hopefully his twin will be too.

Ric was exactly what i needed i cleared my mind and when i was relaxed he took me back home.

I didn't see anyone around so i took the chance and took my Chemistry book and started reading for the test on Friday.

After about an hour the door flew open revealing a very drank Blane.

He came to me and kissed me but i pulled away and helped him to the bed. He was silent then he started yelling all kinds of profanities directed toward his dad.

He talked to his dad last night that might be the cause. But he was okay in the morning. I couldn't help but wonder what exactly his father told him for him to get drank.

CHAPTER 22: New discoveries

My phone's alarm rang waking me up. I went to the bathroom and got ready when i was done i knew that Blane was probably not going to make it to school so i just kissed his cheek and wrote a note.

I went to school text me when you wake up and we have to talk about you coming back home drunk.XX Victoria :)

I went downstairs and has breakfast that Cici prepared we talking a little and she offered to drive me to school cause she was leaving at 11.

She didn't ask me about my mom which I really appreciated cause I did not want to talk about her.

She dropped me off at school and drove off. Walking into the school's hall way I saw Gwen and my first instinct was to turn to the other but when started walking towards me which me mentally sigh.

When she was Infront of me i didn't say a word i waited for her to make a move but she was silent.

"Uhm Can i help you with something Gwen?"

"Just meet me after school not at the smoothie hut I'll send you an address it's really important."

And she walked away and left my head spinning with possibilities.But i just had to wait until we met i guess.

I went to class and pushed away all my thoughts cause i really had to concentrate more in classes.

I needed a scholarship if i wanted to go to college cause my mom wouldn't be able to take care of all the costs or else i could get a student loan.

I was a straight A student i made sure of that ever since my dad left and saw my mom struggle to give me a comfortable life. That's why i couldn't understand why she would want to get back together with him.

Lunch came quick and i grabbed my food and went to our table. I said hello to Brian and Ric but i didn't see Ian. I was beginning to get very worried cause i really wanted to talk to him.

"Where's Ian?" I asked to not directed to anyone specifically.

"Uh He said he was not hungry but he said hy" Brian said but i could see he was lying

"You can just tell me if he is avoiding me?"

"Okay maybe he is. But just give him sometime he needs to adjust "

"Did you tell him Blane and i are official"I asked Ric

He nodded and just then my phone beeped.

Hey Babe sorry about last night. I'll talk to you when you get home. P.s my head is killing meXX your boyfriend ;)

I smiled and replied.

Its your fault your head is killing you I'll buy you some medicine on my way home. See you then XX your girlfriend :)

I put back my phone in my pocket and saw both Brian and Ric looking at me grinning.

"What" i asked asni rolled my eyes.

"I really hope Blane is serious with you cause i can literally see how much you like him by looking at you text him. "Brian said and Ric nodded immediately.

I just smiled and continued with my food.

Finally i got to home and see my boyfriend. Since i didn't have a car Brian said he'll drive me there nad he wanted to have a chat with Blane which is ironic cause i always thought Ian was the one who would go all protective Brother on my first boyfriend but oh well.

We both went in the house and Blane was in the living room but he was with Alex. When did he get here i thought.

"Hey Babe i didn't know you'd be here" Brian said to Alex and he approached him and they shared a kiss they looked a so cute i couldn't help it i took a picture of them.

"OMG you guys are just the cutest thing" i said in a very cheerful voice.

"Not cuter than us Babe" Blane said as he also got up and walked towards me.

I couldn't help but smile like a little girl when he kissed me then quickly pecked my forehead.

I took out the medication i bought on my way here. And he took them without water or even a fruit.

When we were sitting around Brian suddenly asked Blane if they talk privately in his serious voice. He could get scary when he was serious thats why he was always so cheerful but when he was serious he could intimidate almost anyone. But Blane looked unfazed.

He got up and led him to the pool area and it was just me and Alex. It was awkward at first cause we aren't used to eachother but then he spoke.

"You know your the second girl that has ever gotten Blane's attention. But i can tell he really likes you from how he talks about like he's never met anyone like you before. like your this special flower you only find at the top of a mountain."

I would be lying of i said i didn't get jealous when he said the second i wanted to know who was the first person to get his attention.

"I really like him too. Uh who was the first person who got his attention?"

"His childhood bestfriend, Bella ." He said and looked away as if he didn't want to talk about it so i choose not ask any more not because i was not curious but i would just look for an opportunity to ask Blane himself.

We watched tv then my phone beeped. It was a text from an unknown number.

Meet me at the pastry shop close to school in 30 Minutes. Gwen }

I had forgotten about Gwen. I got up and went to change. When i came back down i saw Blane and Brain in the living room again.

"Hey guys i have to go I'll be back in maybe an hour."

"If your going to meet that guy again I'm coming with" Blane said.

"Not I'm not going to meet Coda. No need to get jealous now."

"I'm not jealous. I'm just protective of what's mine and you are mine."

Most people would get made at his possessiveness but i actually find it very attractive And i didn't mind him calling me his. Cause i can also call him mine.

I smiled and went and kissed him.

"I'm meeting a girl so don't worry."

"What if she's a lesbian and want to take you from me?"

"I can assure you she is not. And i have not forgotten we still have to talk. Bye babe"

I didn't want him to know i was meeting Gwen cause he would want to go with me and i really wanted to know what she wanted to tell me. Besides i could handle myself.

I waved by to Alex and kissed Brian on his cheek and went out.

What i got to the little Pastry shop i saw Gwen at the corner. And i went and sat down opposite her.

We said our hellos and i ordered a cup of tea and a donut.

" So what's so important you wanted to talk to me alone?"

"Your dad his name is Logan Martinez right?"

"Yeah as far as I know"

"He is my dad too."

CHAPTER 23: Logan Martinez

"He's my dad too" Gwen said.

I was quiet at first cause she was obviously joking. It was literally impossible.

" Some pranks are very childish even for you Gwen"

"Look Victoria i know i have been horrible but do you think i would joke about something like this. I'm dead serious"

She did look serious but how it was just impossible i would have seen him. But now that i thought about it i have never seen her dad.

"But how? Can just explain it please from the start?"

"Okay. My mom and my Dad were married young but my mom was loaded cause my grandfather is rich so they didn't have money problems. It was all fairies and bunnies until my mom gave birth to my older brother and he got involved with another Woman, your mother. And it was bad she started drugs and what not but then my mom got pregnant again but dad was till with the other woman.

He used to come back home but he doesn't stay long maybe three days then went back. My mom had to suck it up cause she was pregnant she had to take care of herself and my brother. Then after she gave birth to me she thought maybe Dad would finally come back home but he didn't. He stayed away longer but still went back home.

It went on until i was about to turn five. My mom had had enough when she found about that they had a child, you and you even had his name. She was furious so she called Grandfather.

She didn't want to divorce Dad so she just needed Grandfather to scare him into leaving your mom completely. So my Grandfather offered Dad money and one of his companies and he accepted on the condition he loses all contact with you guys not even check up on your guys.

But now mom is worried and she's on drugs again and she's really in a bad state and my Dad is with your mom God knows where?"

I was processing what i just heard the truth about my dad and mom. My mother ruined their family she came in between dad's marriage. It was wrong.

And me. I'm a result of adultery. How could my mom keep this from me. All these years she never thought to tell me oh by the way your dad has another family.

So Logan didn't leave me cause i was fat it was a cover up. He left me for money. He left my mom and I to struggle while he was just handed a company and a shit load of money.

I can't believe how selfish he was. So Gwen is my step sister and she even has an older brother I've also never known about that.

"I'm sorry "

"Why are you apologizing?"

"Cause it's my mom's fault your family had a hard time. I can't imagine how your mom felt?"

"I wouldn't feel so bad it's not like she cared about the family she just wanted him!"

I couldn't understand what she meant. If Logan went back then obviously they are a family again.

"What do you mean Gwen?"

"My mom, she is just as selfish as her husband. Do you know she left us. They moved away both of them but they choose to leave us, My brother and I with a nanny. She said we were in the way of their love. So they moved to take care of the company but they do take care of us financially and they visit for holidays. sometimes."

"Wow am really sorry Gwen!"

"I don't want pity Victoria. I'm very okay with my situation I learned to accept it. But now my mom is back with drugs and everything. I don't care but my brother he's wrapped around her finger and he's stressing and I care about him."

"So what do you want me to do?"

"I just thought you should know the truth cause you clearly didn't and decide whether or not you want a man like him back into your lives cause i know i wouldn't."

She was right I don't want my mom with a man like him.

"Thanks Gwen. But can i ask you a question?"

"Go ahead"

"Is that the reason you were always so mean to me?"

She looked at me at first. Then said"I guess. But my brother recently helped me see your the person to be angry at its all my dad's fault. So I'm really sorry about my behaviour maybe we can even be sisters. I've alway wanted one."

I was taken back by that but Gwen and i are sisters and i don't blame her even i would be mad if my dad had an affair.

"I would really like that Gwen" i said

She smiled and looked at her phone then she said.

"Maybe you could also meet my brother you would love him but now its getting really dark i should get home i live really far."

"Its okay no problem"

We both got up and I paid for our meal and we both drove off.

On the way home i was still thinking about the whole situation it was pretty messed up.

I hated my Dad even more now that i knew the truth. I just needed to realise my anger cause i was pretty angry but i couldn't go off at Gwen since she was also a victim.

I needed to go off on him, Logan Martinez and i couldn't believe i said this but i couldn't wait to see him face to face and let out all my thoughts.

When i got to the house Alex and Brian had already left and Blane had just prepared the table for dinner.

I said hello and sat down i thought about telling him but decided it wasn't the right moment i would tell him on Saturday I myself needed time to accept it all in.

When were finished we washed up and i told him i met Gwen but i assured him we just talked he reluctantly agreed to not asking questions until i decided to talk to him and i really appreciated that.

She snuggled in bed together and we slept but not before i forced him to study with me for the test for at least thirty minutes.

I was very tired mentally and physically so i quickly drifted off to sleep.

CHAPTER 24: Bye Ric

It was Friday the day was almost over. The chemistry test was not hard Blane and I covered most of what was tested. The week was normal Gwen and I said hellos here and there i still had not talked to Ian which really hurt me cause i missed him so much.

We had a four week holiday which i really needed. But my mom was almost coming back from Canada nad i would have to move back in with her and Logan. Don't get me wrong i missed my mom so much but only her not a money loving father coming with her.

Blane and I were sitting on the couch when he held my cheek and kissed me passionately and i reciprocated equally as passionate. He licked my lips and i parted my lips and he took the opportunity and slipped his tongue in my mouth.

I left take control of my mouth as his lips explored all corners of my mouth. His hand moved to my waist and and my shirt while he layed me on the couch and he was on top of me.

We pulled away from the kiss for breathe when he attacked my neck and planted kissed all over my collar bone. When i tried to remove his shirt so that i could feel his abs i heard someone clearing his throat.

Blane groaned as he got off me and i was turned red from embarrassment of being caught. I looked up to see Ric looking at me apologetically.

"Hey Ric" i said as i got up to go to him.

"Hey Tony uhm Ian is in the car he wants to talk. I'll just stay here with Blane" i looked at Blane and he nodded and i went out.

Ian was on the driver seat he was looking better. I got in and sat down and faced him. He surprisingly hugged me and i held in tightly and i let out a breath.

"I'm sorry I was acting like a jerk"

"I will forgive you if you promise not to go this long without talking to me.."

He pulled away and looked in to my eyes and said"I promise and I'm very sorry"

"I forgive you …….. so does this mean your okay with Blane and me?"

"Not completely i still hate him but as long as your happy"

At least he was trying i thought.

"Guess what?"

"What?"

"Gwen's my sister"

He was surprised beyond surprised even then i explained the whole ordeal to him while we aimlessly drove around then we decided to go to get food.

We bought burgers mine, Ian's , Ric's and Blane's. He paid for all of it he said it was an apology .

We drove back home and i convinced him to come in and we can all eat together.

"We're back" i shouted as i got in. Ric and Blane were playing a game connected to the tv.

"Come on lets eat before the burgers get cold"

I gave everyone their burgers and Ian and Blane just nodded at eachother but didn't really speak.

We ate while we made jokes we were all getting along it was nice.

"I'm going to stay with Eva for the holiday" Ric said.

Ric was going to be away for four weeks i was kinda upset i would really miss him why couldn't Eva come here.

"When are you leaving?"

"Sunday"

I know Ric and I weren't as close as Ian cause he was more of a silent brother who didn't say very much but i know he would do anything for me and he never got mad at me even if i acted like a child.

"Well say hy to Eva for us"

"Say hy to your mum too when she comes back and Logan"

We kept on talking until it started getting late and the boys had to go. I told them to say hy to their mom and they left.

Blane and i were in his room just talking while in each other's arms. When my phone buzzed.

Hey our brother really wants to meet you. How about tomorrow same pastry shop. Gwen:)

Blane looked at me questioningly and i replied to the text before telling him the story.

Cool i want to meet him too. Meet you guys then maybe 2pm. :)

I then turned to face Blane who was looking at me clearly waiting for an explanation. I took a deep breath and narrated the story for the second time that day.

"Whoa so Gwen is your half sister and her brother is your half brother and y'all are related and now your dad wants your mom after leaving her for money"

"Well yeah that's mainly it"

"And how are you taking all this"

"Well I've had the whole week to process and I'm okay and Gwen is nice when she is not all mean "

"I guess that's good then "

"Now you have to tell me about the talk you had with your dad "

"It wasn't anything serious its was just about some fantasy he had about the company"

"Okay you sure that's all?"

"Yeah no need to worry"

He said then kissed me. And pulled away.

"We should sleep" he said.

He spooned me and soon enough i drifted off to sleep.

The door bell was insistently being rang so i made my way out of Blane's embrace and when i was about to get out of the door he spoke.

"Where you going Babe"

"I heard someone ringing the doorbell I'm going to check." I said and made my way downstairs.

I hated my sleep being cut short and if it was one of the boys i was going to smack someone on the head.

When i opened the door it was definitely one of them which made me groan and head to living room as Ric followed me.

We said our hellos then he told me he was going to leave to Eva's place that afternoon thats why he came to say goodbye.

I was pissed he woke me up but i had forgotten all about it. He was going to leave me for four weeks. I hugged him and he hugged me back.

"Call me at least once a day."

"I promise i will"

He said as he pulled away and kissed my forehead. Then i saw Blane walk into the room.

I told him Ric was leaving that's why he came to say bye. After a few minutes he left and that was the last i was going to see of him for the next month.

Blane and i cuddled on the huge couch in the living room and i dozed off almost immediately.

CHAPTER 25: Bake

"Baby" Blane said trying to wake me up.

"Ten more minutes"

He laughed and said " your already late wake up"

I finally got up and went to take a shower. When i looked at the time i really was late. We slept till 12:30. I had to meet up with Gwen at 2.

I quickly got dressed in my ripped jeans and one of Blane's huge sweatshirts.

"I'm leaving now" i said.

"Text me when you get there." He said then he kissed me.

I was almost at the pastry shop it was already 15 minutes late. When i got there i saw Gwen alone on the booth at the corner.

"Hey Gwen" i said as she stood up to give me a hug.

"Hey Victoria, my brother when to the bathroom he'll be out in a sec"

"It's okay. How is your mom doing?"

"She's okay i hope we took her to rehab"

"That's nice. My mom is coming back on Monday with Logan."

"Ooh so he finally decided to leave us huh?"

"I for one am totally against it i don't want him being apart of my life again"

"Victoria!"

I heard am all too familiar voice call i turned around and saw the very handsome Coda standing behind me.

"Coda hey" i got up and hugged him we hadn't talked since we meet I kind of missed him.

"Hey uhm why are you talking to my sister?" He said

"We go to the same school.. wait did you say sister?"

I was confused it had never occurred to me Coda could be Gwen's brother. I just stared at Coda when Gwen spoke.

"When i didn't know you too knew each other but Coda this is Our step sister, and Victoria your step brother" she said as she signalled between us.

"Small world huh" Coda said.

We sat down and talked amongst ourselves. I noticed they looked alike if your really studied their features.

"So why exactly were you selling Cotton candy you guys are like crazy rich" i said

"I had a lot of free time on my hands and i decided i can make my own money even though it's not much its mine and i get to meet pretty girl who like me for me just like you not cause I'm from a rich family."

" i guess it worked cause i definitely wouldn't have guessed your from a rich family."

We all laughed and continued to have small talk. Coda really didn't look rich he always this sexy unkept hair vibe and normal clothes no designers unlike Gwen who bought every new Louis Vuitton item that came out. Coda was simply humble and i liked that about him.

I had come to adapt to Gwen. I accepted who she was if she wanted to but every Versace it was her call cause she could afford it and it was who she was. But she was as nice as anyone can be when she isn't bullying you.

She did apologize for that and i accepted her apology.

We talked for a while longer then Coda said he had to leave and he was Gwen's ride so they left but Coda agreed to meet my boyfriend he would drop by in the week that followed.

I left soon after and went back to mansion i now saw as home. When i got home Blane was in the pool showing off his skills.

"Show off!" I shouted.

He still hadn't noticed me watching him until i shouted then he looked at me. He got out of the pool and the water was dripping from his hair to his back and when he turned to face i couldn't control my eyes that decided to roam all over his torso to his V line leading to his manhood.

"Pervert" he said.

Then pulled my eyes from his amazing body and looked at his face.

"Am i not allowed to check out my boyfriend"

"I guess I can't blame you no one can resist staring at all this" he said placing his arms behind his head ehich made his abs much more visible.

"Yeah yeah the Great Blane Saint John cocky as always"

I said as i walked back in the house. I didn't blame Blane if i had his body i would probably show it off too.

His one of those Greek Gods people always speak of if they existed.

I went into the kitchen i wanted to bake while i was gathering the ingredients i needed i felt a pair of mascular arms wrap around my waist. He started kissing my neck. I turned around to face him and immediately our lips made contact.

I moaned but not loud he probably didn't hear it. He grabbed me and placed me on top of the counter but i had stop the make out session before i was actually unable to stop and i pushed him away.

He placed his forehead of mine while we caught our breathe. Then i got off the counter and i heard him groan.

"Want to help me bake?"

"I would love to but i really hate baking"

"I hope you also hate eating cake"

"Now those are two different things"

He said as he left the kitchen to go watch a game that was about to start.

I was in the kitchen for about 2 hours and when the cake was finally ready i cut two pieces and went into the living room.

We silently watched the tv as we ate the cake. I didn't fail to notice that Blane finished his fairly quick.

"This is thee best Cake I've ever eaten!"He said.

"Too bad you don't know how to bake it yourself since you didn't help out"

"How about i help out next time?"

"Yeah okay"

We sat for a while and enjoyed each other's company. Then i took the plate and cleaned up in the kitchen. We were know in Blane's room.

"You can stay with me here if you want to?" He said suddenly.

"But my mom i missed her even though Logan is also coming i want to spend time with her!"

"It's okay but if it gets too much you don't hesitate to come over." He said.

His concern made my heart flutter a little. But what would Adam, his father, think if i just moved in.

So i decided i will look for a job. Even if i had to stay at Blane's place i would at least buy the groceries.

I would start looking for a job the next day. I listened to his soft breathing and i felt very relaxed and it was as if that is where i belonged in Blane's arms listening to his heartbeat. And i drifted off to sleep with a smile on my face.

CHAPTER 26: News

Sunday passed with Blanc helping me pack my stuff. Saying i wasn't very excited wouldn't be a lie cause I wasn't happy about her coming back to a home with thee same man who left us for money.

Maybe she didn't know about the plot, maybe he never told her. I choose to spend the day with Iano we were long over due for a day out and i wanted a distraction. my mom's flight was landing at 10 a.m she called me and offered to pick me up so that we could go home together but I passed up her offer and told her Iano would drop me off in the evening.

ian and I were sitting in his car on a hill top looking the the great view the city had to offer while we ate our MC Donald's burgers. the sun about to set and Ian did try very hard to make me laugh and forget about Logan for a second.

Ian had no plans for the holiday neither did I. I figured Blane and I would just spend time together but Ian and usually spent most of our holidays together so my plan was make sure he got a girlfriend in between.

i wasn't sure how I as going to achieve that since he as very picky but I would try. we avoided discussing my relationship with Blane since i still wasn't sure it was still a soar topic.

After watching the sunset while I must admit was calming we decided to drive around for about an hour then we would drive back home.

As we drove home I choose to let my mom decide what she wanted for herself. if she really wanted to get back together with then I wont be their biggest fans but its her life.

She did take care of when i was little till i was now grown she needed happiness. i mean maybe she wasn't happy with just me in her life.

We finally came to a stop and i saw my house the lights were on. I looked at Ian as I told him I couldn't do it alone.

"Its okay Victoria i'm literally next door if you need me. come I'll go in with you" he said

I let out a deep breathe and finally opened the car door and Ian was right next to me. I walked up to the door and rang the door bell and waited for a minute until the door flew open and revealed a very cheery Mother of mine.

She immediately engulfed me in a hug and I hugged her back and smiled. I pulled away and she lead me into our house. Ian said hello to my mother and when i went into the kitchen then i saw him.

Standing casually in the kitchen as if he lived there all his life.

"Victoria say hy to your father" my mother said.

i took a step forward and held out my hand for him to she shake and he did then I turned to face my mom and said.

"I prefer we call him Logan Martinez not My father" I said very casually.

ian said hello to him and then he followed me to the door since I thought he should go.

"Thanks Ian for a distracting me and stuff" i said as I hugged him.

"if your uncomfortable Ric's room is waiting for you" he said as I pulled away then I smiled at him. He then left after telling my mom bye.

I immediately went to my room. Blane had already brought my stuff earlier. when i wa settled in my bed I heard my phone buzz from my phone.

I miss you. ;)

it was from Blane and I smiled at myself.

I miss you too. ;)

how are you considering the situation?

i'm just going with the flow.

i'm here if you need me :)

I know :) goodnight Saint John.

Goodnight Martinez :)

I connected my phone to the charger took out my laptop and played some music as I tried to sort out my stuff.

I heard a knock on the door and mentally hoped it was my mom not Logan.

" come in" i said.

my mom walked and sat next to me. she asked me about how my four months in Cici's house was. I told her it wasn't great at first but eventually it was great.

"Blane is my boyfriend now" i told her and she looked surprised. even I wouldn't believe me if I said the hottest guy in town was my boyfriend.

we talked about blane and I for a while then I asked her about Logan.

"So you knew he had a family while you had a relationship with hm?" i asked

she looked at her hands on her lap and nodded.

"Mom why would you come in between a family like that?"

"you don't understand Victoria I just fall in love with him it was more than that. it was like we were meant for each other. Like my world started and ended with him. And he loved me back just as much"

I looked at her as tried to understand her feelings.

"Then why did he choose his wife over you then?"

"it wasn't that simple" she said.

"But it was he chose money and a company over you my step siblings that I recently found out about told me everything"

"you've already met then we wanted to introduce you guys ourselves but its okay. how are they?"

"I love Coda and my stepsister used to be my bully why because she blamed me for her family being distant. now stop changing the subject. we both know he choose money over us?"

" they blackmailed him. as you know his Father in law is extremely rich and powerful. since he loved his daughter and a divorce would not look good for him since they weren't married for long,"

" I didn't know he was blackmailed?"

"see that part they don't tell you huh, they told Logan if he left the marriage he would never have a job and everyone would look down upon him he would make his new family surfer. so Logan choose to stay in the marriage on the condition that he was given one of his father in laws company"

"but Logan looked at the bigger picture. he agreed but didn't tell me anything. but his plan all along was to use the company to make a name for himself and create other businesses on his own so that he could eventually be able to come back to me and not have to worry about being destroyed. and it worked he created a name for himself In Canada."

"so now he expects everything to be sunshine and rainbows " I said

" look Victoria can't you see he sacrificed himself for us and he did come back didn't he?"

"so what Mom he wants me to be his sweet little girl again. cause no I remember he when he left he said he left because i was not his child cause he couldn't produce fat children I heard him"

"that was an excuse he used for leaving without me suspecting anything it wasn't ideal but he did what he had to"

"so now what mom he divorces his wife and we live here happily ever after?"

"not here we are officially moving to Canada since his business is there once his divorce is finalized"

"I guess it just going you two there" i said

"Well not for long" she said looking down at her belly and she placed her hand on it.

My eyes widened my eyes at the realisation. Was she telling she was pregnant. They were going to live together as a family and leave me here alone and forget all about me.

I was being replaced while they got a new beginning. A tear fell from my eyes and i wiped it away.

"I'm happy for you" i said then i took my phone and went downstairs and saw Logan on the couch. I went towards him and stood Infront of him.

"I guess your finally going to have your happily ever after without your fat kid in the way. I wished both of you all the luck"

i said as i wiped another tear from my cheeks then quick left the house before he could say anything.

I went directly to Ian's house. And knocked on the door. His mom opened the door ans when she saw me she immediately called Ian.

He quickly came down and came and hugged me while lead me to his room and when i was seated.

I let it all out all the pain when he left. I cried my heart out till i didn't feel anything.

CHAPTER 27: Second chance

"Wake up Tony...."

I groaned and turned and faced the other direction.

"Logan's is downstairs he wants to talk to you!"

I lifted my head to make sure he wasn't joking and he wasn't.

"What time is it" I asked.

"Almost 12"

"Wooah new record. Okay I'll just freshen up and meet you downstairs."

I stayed in Ian's room since Monday evening he brought me food and water he was basically my butler.

It was on Thursday and all I did was eat and watch horror movies with Ian.

I haven't talked to Blane either since i was too lazy switch on my phone well that's what i kept telling myself.

When i took a shower and all clean i went downstairs and there he was. The man who breaks me by disappearing and appearing again.

He watched me walk over and sit opposite where he was.

"Hello Victoria"

"Hello Logan"

I always saw how he usually seemed hurt everytime i used his name to address him.

"I came to over to talk. Your mother said you were angry about us moving to Canada but we only thought you wouldn't want to come with us since your whole life is here your friends I even hear you have a boyfriend now."

"You would have at least asked me if i wanted to come with?" I said i a low voice

"I want you to come with your mother and I. Believe it or not Victoria i want to know you cause your obviously not a five year old girl anymore."

"Obviously" i said

"I'm sorry I left and maybe if i stayed things would have turned out differently. But now i can stay with all of you even the unborn baby and i want all of us.

I want you to be the big sister this baby deserves. I want you to go to any university you wish even if its not in Canada and not worry about not getting that scholarship cause i always kept an eye on you and you are brilliant

I want to know you i want to be your father or at least try to be the father you deserve. If you would let me. I want you to come with us to Canada.

Lets all have a fresh start. I can fly you back every two weeks to meet you friends if you want? What do you say Victoria please think about it"

I let out a shaky breathe. I always wanted a father. Maybe I'm desperate for a father but i did want to try. I wanted a father and i always wanted a sibling.

I stood up from where i sat and went and sat next to him and hugged him. I could see he wasn't in the least expecting that but he hugged me back.

We stayed in our embrace for a few minutes savouring the moment.

" I'm gonna try and give you a chance. And I'll think about moving but if I agree we have to wait till I graduate and let's keep it to ourselves the moving part"

He pulled away and looked at me as if he couldn't believe me.

"I promise i will try to be the father you deserve,"

"Do you love my mother as much as she loves you?"

"I know you think i enjoyed the last years but i didn't I love your mother so much she was always on my mind she was my motivation to keep working and build a future where we would be comfortable i never stopped loving her i never will"

They did love each other alot. I remember every time my mother spoke about him. He adoration of him was literally oozing even when he left she was still madly in love.

That's what i wanted in future a love that consumed me.

"Lets go share this moment with the love of your life then" i said which made him chuckle as we got up.

I called Ian and he came downstairs and i thanked him for the last few days and he said anytime.

We left and walked back to our house. My mom was beaming with happiness when she saw Logan and i holding hands.

I hadn't forgiven him completely but I guess i understood him better his position. And i never realized how i always just wanted a father and when he came back and finally spoke to me i was quick to accept.

We sat in the sitting room Logan and i sharing ice cream. That's were i got my excessive love of ice cream from.

We talked about how they met and how Logan loved throwing me in the air when i was young and it made my mom very angry but apparently i loved it.

This is all i wanted all my life a father who loved my mother and me. Family dinners and talks.

At least the new family edition will have that and i was slightly jealous but i still had them all to myself for a few more months.

My mother was three months pregnant. She would give birth after I graduated.

We talked for a long time when my mom decided we all had to go to sleep. Since she was tired and didn't want to miss anything.

So i was in my room and i decided to switch on my phone.

Disappointed was an understatement. Blane hadn't texted me since he said Goodnight on Monday.

Why didn't he text me to check up on me at least. Ric had called thrice, Brian had left me a million texts even Frank texted me and he was different continent for Christ's sake.

Maybe he wasn't feeling well i concluded . Maybe i should go check up on him. He was all alone he didn't have anyone to take care of him if he was sick.

I suddenly felt guilty cause he could be sick and too self involved to check up on him. So that's exactly what i will do tomorrow. Wake up bright and early and bake him some cookies then go over to his place.

Mom would probably ne asleep when i leave so i decided to go ask for her keys.

I walked to her room and just flew open the door only to find Logan on top of her but not naked which i thanked the Gods for.

"Close the fucking door geez!" I said as i took the keys from the make up table when i had them laugh as i made my way out.

I stayed up for a while and thought about my family. My perfect boyfriend that i really really really liked.

Honestly thinking about it the only people that may hinder me from leaving are my friends, my boys and Blane.

The only boy mental enough to like me apart from my boys and Ian.

CHAPTER 28: Bella

I woke up bright and early went to the kitchen and made one of my best bunch of cookies yet,

I was taking a second shower to relax a bit before going over at Blane's.

I put on some shorts and one of Blane's T-shirt I claimed as ours. I pit my hair in a bun and was ready to go cure my probably sick boyfriend.

I stopped by the supermarket to buy him some of hus favourite snacks and i obviously couldn't forget the ice cream.

It was around 9: 30 when i got close to his place. I know i had been to his house a zillion times i even lived there but i always got amazed by a it.

I parked the car and went in. It was quiet pin drop type quiet. I immediately started heading up the stairs to Blane's room until i saw the TV was on.

I moved towards the living room to switch it off since he probably left it on unknowingly.

Pizza boxes, cans of bier and Soda. I was a surprised Blane was messy but not this messy.

I looked around the living he was no where to be seen so i concluded he was probably in his room and i would clean the mess up later.

I was about to go up the stairs again when i heard laughter. Sounded like wasn't sick at all.

I went into the kitchen. The laughter was still loud but it wasn't one person's. He would be in Blane's house that early morning.

I stopped at the door when i saw Blane on top of a girl they were both covered in Flour looked like they were baking, well trying to.

Obviously he hadn't noticed my presence until the girl stared at me when he turned his head.

The way undeniably beautiful. You know how guys would tell you your the most beautiful women i know well if Blane ever told me that i would hysterically.

She was way past Victoria secret model she was freaking miss world. She had red hair that were wavy and bouncy.

Apart from the girl being gorgeous i was fuming inside. He was having fun with miss pretty face while i was worried sick he might be sick.

He quickly got up and made his way to where i standing. I guess he knew i was furious based on his next words.

"I can explain"

"I bet you can" i said

I moved from my spot but not before looking at miss pretty face and seeing her look at me with a disgusted stare.

I simply rolled my eyes cause i wasn't easily affected by mean stares and words from i don't care about.

I walked to his room as he followed behind me. He locked the door behind him and i was looking around his room i didn't fail to see the girl's blouse his floor.

Blane was my first boyfriend. The thought of him cheating on me would haunt me and that's why i kept pushing the thought a side and that's why i was still composed. Physically at least.

"Her name is Bella"

Geeez even her name means beautiful i thought.

"Go clean yourself up" i said.

"I'll wait for you" i added.

When he went into the bathroom i decided to go talk to 'Bella' for while.

When i got down i heard her on the phone she was talking to someone. Now I wasn't planning on ease dropping but when i heard Blane's name i had to.

"Yeah I'm having fun..... Blane is treating me well he makes me laugh as always......" Before i could hear anymore Blane tapped my shoulder and i mentally groaned.

He led to the pool area to talk. But he just sat as if waiting for me to start.

"I'm Mad" i said

"I know"

"No you don't know. I was worried about you i thought you were sick that's why you didn't call or text. It's like you completely forgot i exist. I woke up and backed you cookies and take care of you. But i arrive not only to see you well and laughing your heart out but with miss pretty face over there."

"I can explain, Bella is a family friend we have been friends since we were kids she spends her holiday in my house sometimes i just forgot to tell you"

"So your just friends"

"Yes that's it"

"So you never in your life had feelings for her as more than a friend"

He was silent. He was thinking about something. Then he finally replied.

"No."

Something was telling me he wasn't telling the truth. But since i heard what i wanted to hear i didn't question it.

"So how long is she staying?"

"Till the holiday is over then she goes back to New York."

I wasn't comfortable about them being alone in the house. But he said they were just friends.

I trusted him. I got upand went towards the pool and took some water and splashed it on him.

"Uh come on i just showered" he said as he stood up.

I started running and he ran after me. Ge caught me like he always did and he was holding my waist and my hands were around his neck as we laughed.

"Do you know how sexy you look when your talking angry" he whispered in my ear.

I lifted my feet moving closer to his lips so that i could kiss him our lips were about to touch until we heard someone clear their throat.

It was none other than miss pretty face. When Blane saw her he tried to move away from me but i pulled him back i saw his smile when i did that and i didn't fail to miss the scroan on miss pretty face's face.

"Hy I'm Bella, I'm Blane's bestfriend" she said with a fake smile and looked at Blane.

"Hy I'm Victoria Blane's Girlfriend, so I'm sure i would have known if Blane replaced Alex as his bestfriend." I siad as i looked at her.

She didn't look happy with the news about me being Blane's girlfriend. But who gave two shits about her opinion.

CHAPTER 29: ART

^^^^ picture of Bella^^^^^^

,
I tried really hard to ignore Bella but she was always there and i wanted to just sit and talk to my boyfriend alone.

So we were in his room scrolling through the TV looking for a program to watch.

Mom called earlier to check up on me if i was good since apparently they were worried.

"What do you want to do?"

"Watch a movie with my girlfriend"

I always got these tiny goosebumps when he called me his girlfriend. It made feel all giddy.

"No i mean college what's your passion?"

"I want to be an artist" he said

That was the last thing that i expected him to say. Who would have thought.

"Why an artist?"

"Cause I'm quite good at it and my mom was loved painting."

"Do you have any paintings around"

He smiled and looked at me the shoved me "come on" he said as he got out of bed.

I followed him without question to a room i never thought to enter. But i was always locked it made me curious but not enough for me to force an entering.

When he opened the door i was in awe. He actually did paint. It was his work room hut some of his art work was on the walls.

I looked at around and spotted this one painting that intrigued me.

It was a man it looked like he was trying to smile but he didn't want to see you'd only notice it if you looked closely. From first glance you'd think it was a stone cold man.

But looking very very closely you'd see. Around the man there was a dark shadow but as if light was trying to penetrate through but was having a hard time.

It was so meaningful but why did he paint it and why was is secluded from the rest of his paintings?

The other secluded picture was of a woman holding a child she had the happiest grin on her face but was also trying to cover the child as if protecting the baby.

I was a fan of art maybe that's why i so observant to the little things.

It turned around and saw Blane leaning by the door. He came closer after a few minutes of staring then pointed to the painting of the woman.

"My mother painted that when she was pregnant with me she wanted to give it to me but never got a chance to."

I could have sworn i saw a tear threatening to fall but just as i saw it it was gone.

I held him and pulled him in for a hug.

"It's okay to be in pain you know" i said

"I know"

He pulled back after a while then he stared at the painting some more.

He then moved to the next one of the man.

"I painted that"

"Why?"

"I feel like it best describes Me i guess"

I just nodded and pretend i didn't just know exactly what he was trying to say in the painting.

He showed others that weren't that significant but still very very beautiful.

"I really hope you become an artist"

"I want to"

"The world really shouldn't be deprived of your art its really beautiful" i said.

"Your the only one who know i want to be an artist not even Alex knows and they've never seen these" he said motioning to the room.

I was special. He was open with me. He wanted me to know him on a very very personal level. And i would be lying if i said that in that moment i was thee happiest woman alive.

After a while of him trying to help me paint something. We went by the pool only to find Bella in a thread she called a swimsuit.

I could see how Blane stiffened at the sight of her in that bathing suit and honestly I just wanted to ripe her to pieces.

Blane was trying to hide how unaffected he was by her but i was able to notice. He excused himself and saud he had to get a drink.

Bella got out of the pool and came towards me.

"See Fat Victoria this..." She motioned to her body "is exactly what a guy like Blane deserves not some over weight little girl"

And before she could move a step farther i grabbed her arm and turned her around to listen to me.

"Listen up Bella. I really don't give a Rat's ass what you think about me ro my appearance. Blane is with me is he not. Despite what you think he actually likes me.."

She started crying like crying crying. What did i do i didn't touch her.

"Why are ...."

Before i could finish Blane was calling my name he sounded angry. I turned and saw him rush towards us.

"Are you okay Bella?"

What the hell? She was being a bitch to me which i refuse to condon anymore. I said i would stand up for myself no one would make me feel inferior again.

"Victoria i said apologize for what you did or said"

RED!!!! All i could see was red. Did he just ask me to apologize to her. She was the one who confronted me. She the one trying to steal my boyfriend.

Oooh i was really infuriated by her. Blane. He was looking at me as if i was a criminal.

"No she doesn't have to do that it okay maybe i really am a Whore" she said as she ran into the house.

What u didn't say anything of that sort.

"Listen Blane i didn't..."

"Just stop Victoria. She is a guest in my house she is one of my closest friends for God's sake and you fucking insult her"

"Jesus just listen...."

"We actually had a moment back there and here you are suddenly insulting my friends"

"Would you just...."

"Maybe she should talk tomorrow i need to make sure she's okay."

And he left me standing there like i didn't matter. He didn't even listen to me for Pit's sake.

I was so mad. I was his girlfriend and didn't even let me talk. He just assumed everything she said was the exact truth.

I was hurt, my heart was hurt. A part pf me was actually begining to believe what she said. Maybe i wasn't good enough for Blane. I mean look at me and look at Her.

Maybe they would make a better couple. I saw how he reacted when he saw her in that thread. Maybe that is what he liked.

And i would definitely never be able to pull something like that off obviously.

I tried to push away the teats that were just about to fall but i wouldn't allow myself to give her the satisfaction of seeing me cry.

I left his house and went straight home. Logan was fondling my mother in the living room and i just smiled said Hello and ran to my room.

How about a sleepover tomorrow would be nice to get to know step sister some more X Victoria ;)

OMG yeees... I'll pick you up at 10 am be ready. Goodnight Step sister ;)

Love the enthusiasm ;) Goodnight:)

Gwen and I had gotten close and we actually had so much in common. We were both Chem nerds for example.

But at the moment i needed her for boy talk which i was in desperate need of.

Guess it had to wait to the next day. And with my puffy red eyes i drifted off to sleep.

CHAPTER 30: Connecting

I woke unexpectedly early on a Saturday. I woke up and did my usual but not in a very happy mood.

I went downstairs for breakfast since i could literally smell the food from my room.

"Hey sweetheart" Logan said.

My mom turned around and hugged me and asked me how my day was yesterday.

"Well it good till it wasn't. By the way Gwen is coming over in an hour am going for a sleepover at her place"

I could see my mom tense but tried to remain calm.

I walked to the other side of the island and took my share of breakfast.

"Logan this breakfast is amazing?"

"How did you know i made it?"

"Cause mom can't cook to save her own life" i said and we all burst into laughter. It felt normal almost natural.

It was my mother's first time meeting Gwen and talking to her. She was a little tense i could notice. But Logan calmed her.

Logan and Gwen were on good terms they talked. Turns out she grew to notice that her dad really wasn't happy hence her mom also wasn't happy.

They talked with Logan and sorted things out i guess. Coda is cool woth anything.

He cares about his mom more and she thought it would be for the best if they split up.

Soon enough we heard a knock on the door. I got up but not before making sure mom was okay.

When i opened the door there she was in just leggings and a Champion hoody and a pair of sunglasses.

She looked nice even without trying.

"Hey sorry i look a mess but i woke up late and just had to rush"

"Are you kidding me you look great... I don't see any mess"

We hugged then ushered her to enter our little family house.

"Hey Princess" Logan said as he stood up to hug her Daughter.

I wasn't even jealous cause i knew he was finally here with me and mom. I had nothing against him and the love for his other children which i thought i would.

The hugged and talked for while until my mom came into view.

"Princess, this is Hali, Victoria's mother"

"Hello Mrs Martinez"

"Please Call me Hali, i feel i should apologize to you for you know" my mother said.

"Oh Hali its okay water under the bridge. If everyone is happy then who am I to go against it"

"Is your mom okay?" Logan said abruptly

"Yeah mom is coping. She is in Rehab but she is making progress"

"That's good i really didn't mean for any of this Princess."

"Its okay Papa, Coda is taking good care of me. He literally the strict mom kids complain about" she said and we all laughed.

Papa, i thought would i be able to call him that also. Maybe one day i might.

I know what you think Gwen is a totally different person. She is. She used to wear the mask painted her to be nad she was happy to play the part ahe explained it to me.

She actually loves cooking and want's to be a Chef when she completes her course in the university she wants to go to.

We stayed for about an hour since mom wanted to know Gwen more and the got along well. Mom even told her to call ger is she wanted to talk to someone and I wasn't available.

We were on our way to her house in her Lamborghini, it was a present from her Grandfather.

Woah.

The house was huge. Scratch that Manor. Apparently it was the Willam's Manor. It were most of the family from far and wide met up for holidays.

It was bigger than Blane's house.

Just like that memories of what happened yesterday came flooding back. And i let out an exaggerated growl.

"Are you okay Vic?"

"Oooh yeah just Stupid Blane"

"Say no more, let me call Brenda and she can prepare for us some massages and you tell me all about it if you want to"

"I want to its why i needed this sleepover"

"Great it will be ready in about an hour i guess"

"No problem. Where's Cuda?"

"Ooh he'll be back by dinner "

"Okay... How about a tour"

"I guess you can see everything in an hour" she said as a joke.

But seriously i didn't think an hour would suffice. The place was just too big.

After an hour of walking around the monar to the tennis court to the outdoor pool and the indoor pool i was just exhausted and that massage just sounded much better.

As were having our massages i told her about Blane and Bella. She listened to me closely and finally said.

"I know people like her they usually get what or rather who they want. But i never thought Blane could be easily manipulated. But in this case he has known her a while so maybe he trusts her that's why. "

"Since they were kids"

"Well then you just have to find a way to expose her what from experience it really really hard cause they always have things planned out. Or wait it out see if she slips up."

" I doubt she will"

"Then dear Sister, if he can't see whats Infront of him and gets manipulated by a fake person leaving a real fantastic person he will be by far thee most stupid person i know "

"Did i tell you how much i love you now"

"Pshh come on girl everyone who has met me, the real me can't help but love me"

We laughed talked, walked down memory lane and ate junk food.

We heard the door open and we both went to say Hello to Coda since he said he was close by. He had no idea i was going to be there so it was a surprise for him.

When we made it to the door we saw a Coda trying to a girl's face off.

"Aarrghhh" both Gwen and i groaned.

He then turned immediately surprised. Then i got a much more clear visual of the girl.

"Stacey!" I said.

Coda looked between us like he was waiting for an explanation.

"Victoria." Stacey said as she jumped me and engulfed me into a literally a bone crashing hug.

"I missed you too but .....i ....need ....to .... breathe" she laughed and let go of me.

"What are you doing here Victoria" coda asked.

"Ooh no hello no i missed you my dear favourite step sister?" I said in a mocking tone.

"I'm sorry you know i missed you i just had no idea. I definitely missed you" he hugged me and most definitely returned it. Then he pulled away and kissed my forehead.

"So how do you too know each other" i asked.

"They like each other but they are both stubborn and don't want to admit it" Gwen interjected.

Well that was new. I'll ask Coda about it later.

"Well okay. Lets go have dinner then. P.s i totally ship whatever you two have going on" i said as i winked at Stacey.

She had gun we laughed and i forgot all about my boyfriend and his new housemate.

I had my own room and yes Gwen said it was mine i was permanently the owner of the room. It was beautiful. I loved it.

When i was all settled and ready to sleep i looked at my phone and sighed. He didn't even check up on me.

When i was about to connect it to the charger i got a call from Ric.

Hey Ric. How are you?

Hey Tony, I'm good. You?

I'm surviving. So what's up with Eva?

INSECURE AND CONFIDENT

She okay. I really like her but she is too wild you know.

You didn't expect her to be perfect did you

Well no but

No so if that's the only thing your uncomfortable with why not talk to her?

I'm scared she might think I'm trying to change her

I think she'll understand if she care about you think. Just tell her to tone it down a bit not get rid of her wild side.

Maybe i could try talking to her.

Good do that. I like that she's wild though maybe you can get out more and not just keep to yourself.

What's wrong with that?

How many friends have you made there so far?

Uh her brother is my friend and her mom.

Your hopeless. Get out make friends your age. Have fun be wild with her a little bit.

Your being a bad influence again.

I laughed.

You know you need me in your life Ric. I'm like your guide to having fun.

Whatever. I gotta go now. We'll talk later.

Goodnight lover boy. I love you and talk to her.

I love you too.

I missed Ric my mood just got a whole lot better talking to him. I didn't want to sleep hit i had to it was too late.

After a some time of staring into the ceiling i fell asleep.

CHAPTER 31: Butt

Yesterday was awesome i really had fun. I was conflicted spend the rest of my holiday in this house or my dad.

And it was Gwen who proposed and assured me i wasn't intruding.

We were in their huge kitchen and Gwen was doing her thing and i was just told to sit and look pretty. I mean i didn't object.

I put on some music and we dancing while she was cooking and i sang very loudly not thinking about the couple in the room.

I mean it was almost noon. I know was the wrong person to judge them but weren't they hungry.

"God can't you listen to music alone the whole damn house can hear!" I heard a very cranky Coda say as he walked into the kitchen.

"I think you've had more than enough sleep."

"I was with a very beautiful woman last night and you wanted me to sleep" He said in a matter of fact voice.

"I never pegged you for a play boy Coda?"

"Well I'm not. I don't bring just anyone around. Stacey is different i really really fancy her."

"Ooowh you fancy her!!!" Gwen and i both sang in an utterly annoying voice just to piss off Coda.

"Shut up she might here you" ge said quietly.

"Why don't you want to tell her?" Gwen asked.

"Cause I don't know if she feels like i do. She can be pretty emotionless you know"

Oh i knew she never showed emotions. She was like an always neutral kinda person and she laughed alot. Not very easy to read cause she acts the same around anyone.

"I think you should try Coda. Or else you'll never know and that will eat you up more" i said.

"Ugh maybe I'll try not today or tomorrow though." He said.

Coda joined in on the singing and dancing till Stacey came and joined us.

It was really fun we were all care free it was the type of fun i hadn't had in a while.

We enjoyed Gwen's food. She said it was her first time making it. But boy did it taste like she had taken classes for that specific dish. It was to die for.

Honestly i wanted Gwen to be my personal chef.

Brenda, was like the head of stuff and took care of Gwen and Coda when their parents were always away.

She was very friendly and asked me to call her Nonna since that's what Coda and Gwen call her.

INSECURE AND CONFIDENT

We spent the rest of day in the outdoor pool cause why not and Coda was literally wrapped around Stacey's finger.

"Coda could you please get me a Soda?" Stacey asked.

"Yes coke no sugar, yes"

"Exactly."

"Whipped" coughed Gwen and Coda gave her a death glare as he quickly went to get her coke.

And we all laughed even Stacey. After a few minutes Coda came back with her drink which made laugh even more and he gave a 'what' look.

I had to go back Home Gwen was driving me back. It was 8 when we started to drive back home. We talked and laughed and didn't even notice how the time had passed by.

She parked out side my house but couldn't go in she wanted to but apparently had something to get to but she agreed to come over for dinner including Coda.

She drove off after telling me and i quote 'don't let Blane bother your pretty little head. If he does i can talk to Coda and he can rough him up' and winked.

I brushed it off and when i was about to get in i heard my name.

"Tony!"

I turned around and saw Ian sitting on his car and waving me over. I placed my bag on the doorstep and went over to him and hugged him.

Normally i would have been scared to sit on his car cause it might dip but since i tried it once and nothing happened i was confident and sat next to him.

He was eating a bad of fries and i gladly stole some from him he didn't mind he was used to it.

"Are really thinking about going to Canada?" He asked suddenly.

"I mean i haven't made a decision but am thinking about it"

"Well if your going I'm going"

I almost choked on my fry when he said that. He was willing to his home behind his family just cause i was moving. It was just absurd.

But knowing Ian he didn't just say that at the spur of the moment. He thought about it thoroughly.

"You can't be serious?"

"I done my research. We both want to be business people and i found a great school. It even in the same city as where Logan's house is. I asked him due to my research."

He was serious. He even found a school. We could both go too he was prepared. We always talked about going to the same university but i wasn't in my head that much.

"Your really serious huh?"

"Victoria where you go. I go. Where i go. You go. It works like that. And i won't allow us to drift apart just cause you moved and i could have easily stopped it"

"I love you so very very much. But you know we can never drift apart right?"

"I don't want to take my chances"

"What about your family"

"Your also my family Tony and i know Ric will always be busy with his girlfriend since he wants to go to university over there and I'll be alone. Brian has his boyfriend"

"Its me and you against the world then" i said.

"Always had been always will be."

We talked about everything. And laughed about how we always wanted to live together when we get to university.

We wanted to rent this house and we would all pay rent together and have lots of fun. I guess it won't happen anymore.

"So have you told Blane?"

I mentally groaned and my heart tightened when i thought about what he could be doing with Bella at that exact moment.

"Uh told him what?"

"About you know Canada?"

"No because I'm still not sure about Canada"

"Do what you want. You've always wanted a family and you finally have that. Whatever you choose i support you 100%"

"Thanks Ian. I literally have no idea what i would do without you"

"You would be a depressed teenager with no one to talk to" he said

We laughed and stayed outside and watched the stars for about an hour till i phone rang. It was mom asking if i choose to stay in Gwen's place some more.

I decided i should just go inside and we'll talk later.

Ian watched go back in the house as he stayed outside.

I couldn't help but think about what he said. He felt alone. I know he was talking about the future but i thought maybe he was actually talking about that moment.

"Hey sweetheart" logan said as he came in for a hug. I gladly returned it.

We watched TV together and Logan told me about my mother's cravings in the middle of the night when she was pregnant with me.

She would ask for Bbq Sauce in the middle of the night. It was the craziest thing i heard of and laughed till my ribs started hurting.

Even with the distraction Ian was on my mind did he really feel alone. I went to my room later and decided to text Ian.

Hey come over. Secret sleep over, I'll let you spoon me ;)

Do i bring ice-cream or you'll provide ;)

Just get your butt over her!!

Didn't know you missed my butt so much. Look down your window;)

I laughed and got up to see him standing outside bent over showing me his butt.

"Freak cover your ass you pervert!!"

He lifted his short and brought them back to his waist and climbed up my window but i stopped him before he got in.

"What Tony. I promise i brought my butt with me"

"Urgh just get in here"

He got in and sat with me on my bed. We talked for hours and laughed at my favourite series FRIENDS .

"Thanks Tony"

"What for?"

"Telling me to come over here"

"Your just here cause your butt couldn't bring itself."

He laughed loudly i had to smack him to remind him my mom didn't know he was here.

"Your welcome"

We spooned like old times and slept like Babies.

CHAPTER 32: Drinks

Ever felt like someone was staring at you yeah that's exactly how i felt.

I fluttered my eyes open trying to adjust to the light and there he was in all his glory, Ian.

"Ugh your face not the first thing i wish to see when i wake up!" I said groggily.

"Well i guess you'll have to deal with it. Btw your boy toy is downstairs waiting for you?"

"What!"

"I said your boy..."

"I heard what you said bafoon. What is he doing here?"

"He said he wanted to talk to you but i told him your sleeping and i wont wake you up till you wake up on your own"

"How long has he been here?"

"Uh not long about an hour"

I groaned and got out of bed. I quickly brushed my teeth took a quick shower and put on sweatpants and a shirt. Then i went downstairs.

Mom and Logan were on on couch cuddling which they seemed to do alot.

"Hey mom, hey Logan"

"Hey sweetie" they said in unison.

I went into the kitchen not saying hello to Blane. I did see him on the other couch but u was still pretty mad.

He walked into the kitchen and stood at the entrance. I took a cup and made some tea.

"Hey Martinez"

"What do want Blane?"

"Can we please talk"

I didn't say anything and walked past him and started heading back to my room. He was following me.

I sat on bed and waited for him to talk.

"I can we just forget about what happened"

"That's all you came to say?"

"I'm sorry"

I looked at him he did look apologetic but he was still living with her. I might trust him but her never.

This was exactly what Bella wanted Blane and I to fight. And last i wanted was for her to actually get her way.

"Do you at least believe me when i say i didn't call her a whore. And i did i trust i wouldn't deny it "

"I believe you"

He came towards me and sat next to me and held my cheek caressing it.

"Am I forgiven?"

"I guess"

He leaned in and kissed me. It was rough but passionate as well and very demanding. He moved his hands from my cheek to my waist pulling me closer.

He laid me down on the down as he bit my lower lip making me gasp and he took the opportunity to slip his tongue in mouth. Our tongues moved in synch.

He door suddenly burst open and there she was, Bella. I looked at Blane with an unbelievable expression.

"I told you to wait in the car Bella what don't you understand?"

"We are already 2 hours late for the party come on.." she whined.

"What party?" I asked almost immediately.

"Some friend of mine wanna come along"

I heard sigh from behind obviously not happy about the invitation Blane just extended.

"No sorry I have to read i kinda behind with my schedule"

"Nerd" Bella coughed.

I rolled my eyes and focused back on Blane.

"Okay then I won't go either?"

"What!" Bella literally screamed.

"I never really wanted to go you did so here are the car keys. Have fun"

He gave a death glare if they actually worked i would be six feet under.

He grabbed the keys from him and stormed off.

"So how about we try some chemistry" he said wriggling his brows and leaning in for a kiss. I turned my face and he kissed my cheek.

I got up and went downstairs.

"Hey Sweetie I'm taking your mom put for dinner then we'll spend the night at a hotel we'll be back tomorrow evening"

"See what men are doing for their women Blane" i said sarcastically

"Its okay have fun"i added

Well i guess they wanted privacy to do stuff. The thought of it made me cringe. But i didn't blame my mom, Logan was a physically fit for someone his age.

We sat down on the table as i quizzed Blane then i heard a knock on the door. I opened the door and Alex and Brian were standing on there with drinks.

"Hy Alex and Brian i said as i hugged both of them. Then they let themselves in.

"Not that am not happy to see guys or anything but what are you doing here?"

"Blane texted as to come over with drinks. Here we are!" Alex said.

I gave Blane a stare and he immediately came towards me "come on, Babe just a little fun"

"Please!!!" The all literally begged.

"Uh why not. Where is Ian?"

"He'll be right over" just as Brian finished speaking Ian badged into the house with a bottle of alcohol.

It was going to be a long night.

After the shots i was also forced to take i was a little tipsy but i could understand what was going on.

We just sitting around talking when Brian decided it was good time to ask

"Tony have you ever thought about marriage?"

"Yeah i want no part of it" i said truthfully.

"Why?"

I just shrugged which apparently made him more interested when i thought he had given up.

"Lets truth or dare... If you cant answer or do something your paying up" he said.

We sat in a circle and it stopped on Ian and he was choose dare hence him giving me a lap dance which i admit was the funniest thing i have ever seen him do.

After a few rounds it finally landed on me i choose truth cause God knows what these drunk teenagers would ask me to do.

"Why don't you want to get married?"

I should have known that was coming. Well i didn't want to pay up but again i was ashamed.

"Cause I'm scared no one will want to marry me and hence I don't want to expect or dream about something that might never happen. Get it now" i shouted rather than answer his question like a normal human being.

I quickly got up after my outburst. Lucky me Blane wasn't there to witness me being pathetic and in my feelings.

Who was i kidding i did dream about my wedding, my family a husband but i know there was a high possibility that it might not happen so i just resorted to making people think I didn't want it.

Blane walked into my room and spooned me but didn't say a thing. So we just stayed in comfortable silence.

I mentally happy danced when he didn't ask me a question cause i wasn't one to openly admit my fears.

I turned around and looked at him he was already asleep and his light snores were music to my ears.

After watching him for a while i got up and went downstairs knowing i had to clean up but when i got there everything was already clean not a single can on the floor and the boys on the couch already asleep.

I took a picture of Alex and Brian while they cuddled on the couch together just like i had with Blane i wasn't able to resist. I also took one of Ian then i took a blanket and covered him since he didn't have anyone to cuddle with.

I kissed their foreheads and went back to my room. I stared at my boyfriend and wondered how long would it last. I didn't care, i knew it wouldn't last forever but i would make the best of the time i had with him then.

When i was about to fall asleep i heard him say something. I turned back to look at him, he was sweating alot.

"Madre.... Madre.... Madre...." He kept on saying Madre. It was Italian i knew some of it but not alot but i was sure he was calling his mother.

I shook him a little to wake up then he did. He was breathing so heavily. I hugged him and assured him he was dreaming until he calmed down.

He was able to go back to sleep which meant i could also sleep but i was still worried about him but i would wait for him to tell me.

CHAPTER 33: hanging

My eyes fluttered open, when i got well adjusted to the sunlight my eyes met Blane's chest. It was the best view to wake up to.

I moved further so that i could see his face. My hand fingers traced is face it well defined he perfectly sculpted nose. His face that fell to his forehead. He was beautiful. He opened his eyes and looked at me and i quickly remove my fingers from his face.

"Don't stop admiring me on my account"

"And the cocky dumbass returns"

"You wound me Babe!" He said looking hurt.

I shrugged and got up and went to the bathroom. I did my normal routine and quickly got out. I let Blane freshen up as i went to make some breakfast.

"Hey boys" i said as i saw them sitting in the kitchen.

The said there hellos and looked at me.

"Okay what do y'all want for breakfast?"

"Pancakes would be nice" Ian said very quickly.

"Ian make Coffee for everyone I'll get to the pancakes"

"Why do I have to do it?" Ian asked

"Cause i said so now get to it"

I gathered the ingredients and started mixing them in a bowl. Soon Blane came down all fresh but busy on his phone.

"What are you doing I asked?"

"Remember the chemistry test we did on a Friday before the holidays?"

"Yeah?"

"They just sent the results i got a A-" he said.

"Congratulations Blane."

"Well its all thanks to you and all the pushing and helping me study"

Blane wasn't bad in school he was an average which is not bad. Ian also an average. Ric was as good asni was but i was better. I took out my phone to look at the results.

"What did you get Martinez?" Blane asked.

"Uh A-" i said.

"Damn, my girlfriend is like smart smart"

"My boyfriend is smart smart too" we both laughed.

I was blessed with a brain which i intend on using to grow a business i want people to know me for my great work ethic and success thats why i study so much i want to make a name for myself.

Ian got a B- , Brian B and Ric got a B+. Blane was smart but had to read to pass but I read to remind myself cause whatever was taught by the teacher sticks so I usually do not need to back to it.

"Would you go on a date with me Tomorrow?" Blane asked suddenly.

I won't lie and say my heart rate didn't increase cause it did.

"I would love to go on a date with my boyfriend. Anyday, anytime anywhere." I said as he held me pulling me closer to him.

We were Kissing when the boys came into the kitchen for the pancakes that were already served.

"Come on people eat here" Ian said pretending a gag. I rolled my eyes and pulled away from him.

We sat and ate together as we made jokes and laughed about literally everything.

I was happy no one remembered my little over reacting about marriage cause they were pretty drunk.

After the boys cleaned the kitchen since I cooked we were all sitting in the living room watching some movie I wasn't really paying attention to.

"Babe i gotta go?"

"Why" i whined.

"Well, Bella is probably trashing my house and i really love that house so I'm gonna check up on her. I'll pick you up tomorrow at 5 p.m. Good?"

"Perfect" i said with a smile as i escorted him to the door.

Then he suddenly remembered he didn't have his car since he gave Bella the keys.

"Alex get up nad drive me home!" He literally commanded him.

"A please would be polite but since you don't know the meaning of the word. Let's go"

Blane gave him his award winning smile as his dimples showed and his very white teeth.

"I'll come back and pick you up when I drop off this asshole." Alex said to Brian. Before kissing him on the cheek.

I loved gay couples there was something that fasinated me about them and everytime i saw them showing affection for one another i could help but explode on the inside.

Blane kissed me on my forehead and left with Alex.

Ian, Brian and i decided to call Ric and check up on him so after overwhelming him with our stupid questions we let him go back to his girlfriend.

He did talk to her and she understood him which i knew she would. I still haven't talked to her in person so I don't have a solid opinion on her yet.

Alex came back an hour and a half later to pick up his boyfriend and it was just Ian and I.

I got and incoming call so i picked up the phone.

"Hello sweetie"

"Hey mom, you guys on your way home?"

"Yeah we are i just wanted to check up?"

"Really since yesterday you just now decided to check up?"

"I was caught up in something" i heard giggles in the background and decided to ignore what my mind was deriving to.

"We were asking if you wanted some Chinese?" She asked

"Of course I want Chinese food. "

"Okay Honey be there in an hour. Bye"

She hung up. Ian said he wouldn't stay for dinner since his mom wanted them to eat together so he was just keeping me company till they arrive.

After making jokes and passing time they finally arrived and Ian said hy and went to his place.

My mom and i set up the table and we all sat to eat.

"What did you do Mi amor?" Logan asked.

"Well Blane, Ian , Brian and his boyfriend stayed over we had fun."

"How is Brian I haven't seen him in a while?" My mom said joining the conversation.

"He said hy and he misses you. He has a boyfriend , he is Blane's friend, they are very cute together."

"That's so nice sweetie and Ric where is he?"

"He went to visit his girlfriend" we noticed how Logan felt left out and mom explained

"Ian you've already met has a brother Ric they are brothers. Brian the one with the boyfriend and there's Frank who is in Germany right now, They are Victoria's Best friends. They literally grew uo together and their parents and good people too"

"I've met Ian he seems like a nice young man I've yet to meet the rest" he said "you don't have female friends?"

"I do like two or three. I don't get along with females alot"

"Hmm" he said as he kept on eating his food.

We sat in silence for a while as we ate when i remember i had to tell my mom I was leaving the next day.

"Mom I'm going out tomorrow at 5." I

"Where to?"

"I don't know. Blane is taking me on a date."

She looked up at me with such excitement you'd think she was the one going on a date.

"Can i help you dress up and do your make up. I've always dreamed of doing these things but your always so not into it" she looked at me with ao kuch hope i couldn't say no.

"Uh okay mom we can play dress up" i said to make her happy.

She gushed and started talking about how she always dreamed of this day. Rolling my eyes I got up and cleaned the dishes and went to my room.

I got a message notification.

I can't wait for our date tomorrow X Blane;)

Speaking of which what should I wear?

Anything maybe a dress we are going for dinner.

Okay. How's your house?

We passed out in the living room so she didn't get a chance to mess it up.

And you owe it all to alcohol. Haha

I guess I do. Goodnight Martinez:)

Goodnight Saint John:)

CHAPTER 34: Dress up

"Wake up sweetie" my mom said for the twentieth time.

"What time is it?"

"Ten on Thursday"

"Its too early leave me alone"

"I pour cold water in you if you don't wake up in 10 minutes"

I groaned and woke up. I understood this was a very exciting day for her. She finally gets to play dress up with her only daughter.

I got dressed in my usual trousers and a shirt and went downstairs. I took some toast and started eating.

"Where are we going to?" I asked.

"We have a manicure and pedicure appointment the best in the city then we have to go to the saloon also the best hairdresser in the city but first dress shopping."

It all sounded so expensive. I immediately knew that Logan was paying for all of it. Not that we couldn't afford it without but we weren't the go the best hairdresser in town kind of people we were the normal hairdresser is good as long as its a reasonable price.

It was cause some serious damage to my mom's bank account.

"Thanks mom" i said then she left the room to take her purse from her room.

"You know you don't have to pay for all this" i said directing it to Logan.

"I wanted to I've already missed enough chances to spend on my daughter but not anymore and don't spare any expense"

"You don't have to make it up to me" i said.

"I want to."

"Thank you"

"How about you thank me by spending a day with me maybe Wednesday"

"Yeah i would love that."

"Let's go. Bye Love" mom said.

We left the house and went to the mall for shopping. I could feel the excitement oozing from my mom its all she could talk about on our drive.

We went into a store it didn't look like i store i could afford anything in but she insisted. She picked a few dresses for me to try on.

Wearing and removing clothes was the part of shopping i hated but i would do anything for my mother.

The dresses weren't bad. I didn't hate them like i thought I would which was surprising.

After trying on a dozens of dresses from different stores she forced me to by some underwear in Victoria secret. I mean the little pieces of clothes were expensive.

Not like i would were thongs unless it suited my clothing i thought they were very uncomfortable.

Yes i did wear granma panties and they were comfortable. And that's all that mattered.

I also bought a bikini cause it really looked nice, not that i would wear it anytime soon but i felt like i would one day.

We were now having manicures and pedicures it was kind of relax we sitting side by side listening to the music in the background.

"How was it in Canada?"

"How do you mean Honey?"

"Did you like living there? "

"Yes Honey i really do and ypur father's business is really good and improving. He left someone in charge so that he wouldn't be distracted when he was getting to know you"

"we are spending the day together on Wednesday"

"That's good. I really appreciate you trying it means a lot"

"He is my father after all right"

She smile. I knew she was happy. She always wanted a family so do I but to build a relationship a strong one will take time. And I'm ready to try.

We finished the pedicures then went to the saloon. The hairdresser was well known even worked with some celebrities.

INSECURE AND CONFIDENT

She did my hair in a nice up do and i liked how i looked. I didn't want to apply make up cause i was messy and would eventually ruin it. Also because i liked how i looked.

After we had done everything we went back home. It was around 3 when we got home. Logan was watching a movie she we got there.

She turned to look at us. My mom had also done her hair and make-up i had no idea why but i didn't ask.

"You look beautiful Mi amor" he said to my mom. Well i didn't blame him. My mother was beautiful and she also wore a dress we bought she was all dolled up.

"Oh so I don't look Beautiful cause I'm in a sweatshirt?" I said. I was joking.

"No no nino you are always beautiful since you were a baby"

I think i blushed a little.

"I was joking" i said laughing and quickly went to my room.

Well i was exhausted i thought about having a quick but i knew i would over sleep and i didn't want that. I texted ian.

Iano..??

Tony..??

Where are you?

I'm hanging out at Brian's you weren't home whenni came by. Why?

Oh okay. I was just asking. Have fun X !)

Have fun on your date. Use protection ;)

I'll keep that in mind.. say hy to your butt. X ;)

Do you want a butt pic I don't mind really ;) haha

Bye dumbass. :)

It was four thirty so i had to get ready. I went to the bathroom and took a quick shower and got dressed.

I wore a white dress that my mother had told me try on and i fell in love with it.

We also bought heels but very low since I wasn't able to walk in them it would be my first time.

I wouldn't have made a big deal of this date if not for my mom.

I took a purse and went downstairs to wait to my date.

My mother and Ligan were on the couch when they heard me they all turned.

My mother approached me first.

"My baby is grown up" she said teary.

"You look gorgeous nino " Logan said and he engulfed me in a hug.

They kept on telling about how grown up i looked and beautiful until we heard the doorbell.

It was as if the doorbell made me nervous cause that's exactly how i was.

Blane had never seen me all dolled up and dressy and i was scared of his reaction. Maybe he preferred how i usually looked. Maybe he wouldn't like how i looked and cancel the date.

Breathe.

Breathe.

I kept on telling myself that as Logan went to answer the door.

I followed behind him and when he opened the door he was wore black and a brown jacket.

He looked so handsome. When his eyes landed on me he had the same expression i had like we've seen anything more perfect. Its like my mom and Logan weren't right there.

"Be careful" Logan said.

"Mmh" Blane responded..he wasn't even paying attention until Logan tapped him in the shoulder and whispered something in his ear when he tore his gaze from me.

"Uh can I bring her back tomorrow?" Blane asked.

"Yeah Honey have fun and be safe" my mother quickly answered when Logan looked like he was about to decline his offer.

I looked at Logan to try and reassure him it was okay then he nodded.

I stepped out of the door and closed it behind me. We walked to his car and stopped at the passenger door.

He immediately brought his lips to mine and kissed me. It was sweet not fast like he was commemorating the moment the pulled back. I followed him wanting more which made him smile and lean in to my ear.

"Your beautiful Martinez. Your perfect" he said.

I was past pink cheeks i was way over red. He was being sweet but at same time incredibly seductive.

I cleared my throat and said thanked him. He opened the door for me then went to his side and got in.

CHAPTER 35: Business Woman

Blane's Pov

We were in the car driving to the destination of our date i was planning on surprising her after we had dinner.

She was sitting right next me looking exquisite as ever. The dress really complimented her figure it was almost impossible to concentrate on the road but i didn't want us dead so i had to.

I placed my hand on her thigh to maybe at least replace looking at her but it just me aroused to a point i had to move in my seat so that she wouldn't notice.

I saw her stiffened and blush at the sight of my hand on her thigh and i loved it. How she usually reacted to me it showed me the effect i had on her and i loved it.

I did have an effect on alot of girls even women over my age but who could resist me. But i didn't want any of the nearly as much as i wanted Victoria.

I knew she wasn't happy when Bella made an appearance even I didn't expect her.

Bella, my childhood friend, i actually thought we would end up together that's why three years ago i asked her to be my girlfriend.

Ahe gave me some crappy excuse saying she didn't want to ruin our friendship and shit like that. I thought i was hurt broken hit i soon learnt that we wouldn't have been a good fit.

She drinks alot and loves parties i do too but not as kuch as her i like it once in a while. She has slept with Sam on several occasions, i didn't know about that until i told Sam about my supposed heart break.

She was spoilt and I'm actually happy she turned me down i really wouldn't have been able to open up to her like i do with Victoria.

I know i messed up when Bella pretended to be insulted by Victoria i should have read through her it wasn't her first time putting on an award-winning performance.

I knew she was pretending when i went in after her and she tried to make out with me. She kissed me at first and i admit i did kiss her back and he kind of made out which i regret alot and i swear on my Mother's grave i didn't mean to.

I still had little feelings for her she was gorgeous anyone would but as soon as i came back to my senses i pushed her off and left to Alex's house.

I know i should tell Victoria about it but i won't happen again so what she doesn't know wouldn't hurt her would it?.

I pushed any thoughts of Bella from my head i was going on a date with my girlfriend who looked like a freaking God and Bella was just making me pissed off.

We got the restaurant and i told to wait in the car so that i could open the door for her. Part of the charm.

I held put my folded arm our her her to intertwine her arm in mine. We were dining at an expensive restaurant it was owned by Sam's father he owned a chain of well known restaurants so i got an easy reservation.

I removed my coat and and left at the reception area. I when we were ushered in and the lady showed us to our seats that were a little distanced from the rest.

I could see how she was looking around in awe and excitement. I couldn't but grin for being the reason she was so excited.

"This all looks really expensive?" She said suddenly.

"Yes it is" i said as i watched her look at the menu.

"I don't think i carried enough money to pay for it I'll have to use my dad's credit card and i didn't want to"

"Why would I ask you on a date and let you pay i thought you were brighter than that Martinez" i said chuckling.

"I brighter than your dumbass" she retorted.

I laughed before replying. "I thought you would be nicer to me considering you dressed up for me" i said winking at her.

"If it was up to me i would just throw on the first thing i saw in my closet"

"Then you would feel underdressed and be all embarrassed since i would look much more sexier than you but in this case i feel underdressed and you are definitely sexier" i said the last part in a low tone.

"So your saying I'm out of your league" she said with a smirk on her face bit i could see she was trying to hide her blush by acting confident.

The waiter appeared and took our orders and said it would be ready in fifteen minutes.

"You never told me what you want to do career wise?" I asked

"Business"

"Why?"

"I think i would be good at running a business and it's my dream to be a very successful well known business Woman. I want to be the woman men take a week to prepare when they have to meet me."

"I think you would make a magnificent business Woman and i want to be right by your side when you take over the business world. "

I saw her face drop for a minute before she tried to play it off. I shrugged it off Maybe it's not what i saw.

We talked about random stuff and i have always felt impeccably happy just having a conversation with the girl sitting Infront of me.

Our food came and we ate till our plates were clean and stayed for a little while till we decided the food had settled and we go on our way.

"Are we going to your place?" She asked she sounded not so excited.

"No Mi amor" she blushed at the name but i could see she was happy we weren't heading home.

She either didn't want the night to end or didn't want an encounter with Bella. Either way she wanted to stay with me felt like a puppy playing fetch. Happy.

CHAPTER 36: Puppy Blane

Victoria's Pov

"Are we going to your place?" I asked not wanting to go back yet.

"No mi amor" he said and my insides flipped.

Earlier Blane said he wanted to help me achieve my dream of being a successful business woman but i still wasn't sure whether I'll be staying or going to Canada.

Blane still wasn't aware about my mom's pregnancy and that Logan asked to also move to Canada. I wanted to tell him but it's as if I'm waiting for something.

I need reassurance if i choose to stay he will always be with me. I'm not expecting a proposal or anything but just something to make me be a hundred percent sure i would sacrifice my chance at a family finally and stay.

I was falling head first for Blane and i was scared, terrified even I didn't if he felt the same way.

I stopped worrying about Bella cause i trust him. He wouldn't do anything to hurt me and i didn't need to worry. She was just intimidating and not what i wanted to think about.

I turned and looked at Blane he was concentrating on the road but had a faded smile.

I looked as his face every single detail about him was enticing his sharp jaw and his hair that was curly from a far and his muscles that were very well fitted in the shirt.

He looked at me and smirked clearly he saw me admiring. But i didn't shy away i smiled.

"Where exactly are going?"

"Relax I'm not kidnapping you or anything."

"Clearly i would beat you black and blue"

He laughed like a rib hurting kind of laugh.

"No one says black and blue anymore Martinez"

"I'm an old soul and didn't you hear tye part where i threatened to beat you up"

"Come on Martinez i know you would never do anything to hurt me you like me too much"

"Keep telling yourself that" i said as I rolled my eyes.

We soon came to a stop and i immediately remembered the place. He took me back to his treehouse. Which i loved by the way.

It was decorated in lights and the was a pickup truck parked and a whole set up behind the truck.

"What's all this?" I asked

"Part two of the date. Come on" he sai as he led me closer to the truck.

The back of the truck had a blanket and pillows and he really worked hard to pull off all these. The pillows must be new and the truck where did he get it.

I turned and hugged him as tight as i could repeating thank you after thank you. Till i pulled away.

"Really Blane thank you it's really beautiful where did you even get this idea?"

"Promise to not think any less manlier of me". He said as he looked away

"Depends now tell me"

"I always wanted to do this cliché stuff with someone i mean i laugh at it with my friends in movies and stuff i secretly also want to remove my jacket and give it you" he said as he scratched the back of his head.

It was the cutest thing I've ever heard.

"God! your such a puppy in the inside" i said as i held his face. And he grinned.

"And i love it! You can do all the cliché stuff you want with me anytime" i said and i kissed him lightly.

"Oh I'm planning on it" he said before he pulled me by my waist and smashed his lips on mine.

After he made out for a short while we sat on the truck and snuggled as we were about to watch a movie.

"Which movie is it?" I asked

"Beauty and the beast"

"Really a Disney movie?" I said as i laughed

"Yes a Disney movie i love beauty and the beast"

"You are such a girl " i said as i lightly hit his chest.

"I thought I was a puppy?"

"My puppy"

"Damn right. Now shut up the movie's starting"

And that was my queue to shut up and i did. I watched a Disney movie i wasn't a fun before but i definitely was now.

I liked this side of Blane so care free and childish like he didn't have a single worry on earth.

I snuggled in closer and he gladly pulled me closer and wrapped his hands around me.

We watched the movie till the end and i loved it. Yes, it was my first time watching it. I can't be blamed i was always with boys and they fancied animé to Disney movies. Brian was a sucker for fairytales though he probably watched it.

We talked for a while it was almost 11:30 pm.

"Remember the first time you brought me here?"i asked

"Yeah how could I forget you loved alot i knew you'll love to come back."

"So what will happen to your treehouse when you move away or something?"

"Well, I plan on retiring early around 45 and coming back i want my children to grow up here and i will give the treehouse to them" he said with a huge smile on his face like he was imagining his kids playing around the treehouse.

"That sounds really good Blane"

"I know, i want to give them every single thing their little hearts desire. I want a girl and i will treat like Princess she will be" he said again.

I couldn't help but look at him with admiration of how he dreamt of a future family. A part of me imagined me being his wife and our kids running around and our daughter being a daddy's girl.

I know i was thinking very far ahead but i couldn't help it. I wasn't even eighteen yet. But i will turn in a few weeks.

We talked about what we envisioned our futures for hours on end and we fell asleep on the truck.

CHAPTER 37: Family

I woke up when i felt the sun rays. I groaned and tried to open my eyes and getting adjusted to the light.

Blane was still sleeping like a baby on one of the pillows. Yesterday was amazing i mean i haven't been on that many dates but even i did that still would be the best date in my books.

After a very eventful day of eating away our joy and switching off our phones, after talking alot of goofy pictures, so that we could live in the moment as he so well put it.

Blane was driving us back we had to go to his first so that i could change into normal clothes.

We noticed the cars parked outside. We walked in and immediately went into the living room since we heard laughter.

Mr and Mrs Saint John and of course Bella. They were all holding drinking and talking then Blane cleared his throat to get their attention.

The first to turn was Cici and she immediately got up to hug Blane.

"Ooh Baby i missed you so much. You know it wouldn't hurt to call me more than once in three weeks"

"I missed you too Cici, i will call you more often." He said as he hugged her back.

They and Cici immediately asked me to sit down after she also gave me a hug.

Adam, Blane's father just nodded in his son's direction and so did Blane.

It made me think about my relationship with my father i definitely didn't want just a nod fron him i wanted love and i was happy he was back although I was hard at first what did they expect he did leave.

"How is your father's business Bella?" Adam asked.

"It's going really well he really is looking forward to the union it will be beneficial to both companies." She answered.

That was my queue to leave.

"I should go change and i can call Ian to come pick me up" i Whispered to Blane and got up.

On my way up i switched on my phone and called up Ian.

Whatchu need Tony?

Can't i just call you and just say how much i love you.

Haa.. come on spit it out Tony

Mpph... Can you pick me up at Blane's and i love you so much

Your lucky i was on my home from somewhere not far from there. Wait for me outside in 10 minutes.

Great see you in ten. X

I hung up and took the clothes i left behind incase i ever slept over. I took a shirt and a pair a jeans i really wasn't a fan of and put my dress in a bag and Blane's clothes that i was wearing.

I was going down the stairs and i saw Blane waiting for me. He wasn't happy but he usually never was with his Dad around.

"Ian will be here in 3 minutes I'm going to wait for him outside"

"Let's go then" he said, he tried to smile but it didn't reach his eyes. I leaned in and kissed him.

I saw Bella looking at us bit not with her normal bitter look. She looked as if she knew something i didn't. I pushed my feelings aside and went outside woth Blane to wait for Ian.

"What are you doing tomorrow?" Blane asked.

"I'm going with my mom to the doctor" i said.

"Why are you going to see a Doctor?"

I had forgotten Blabe had no idea about My mom's pregnancy and the offer of going to Canada.

"Just a check up" i said

Before Blane could question more Ian's car was Infront of us.

I kissed Blane and got in Ian's car. I waved at Blane as Ian drove off.

"How was the date?" Ian asked.

"Good"

"Really good" i added.

"Thought about Canada yet? Cause we need to apply for schools we graduate in two months Tony"

"Yeah i know i just don't know yet"

"I think the only thing that is a hindrance to your decision is Blane. But you can't base your entire future on a high school crush. Blane's father is wealthy he inherits companies even if he moved to Africa. You Tony have to work hard, your future is not certain, or mine but his is since he was born he is the heir to the Saint John companies. I think you should go with the family you've always wanted and make a name for yourself. Your still young and you shouldn't base your huge life decisions on a boy. You should base your decisions on what you think is best for you. Think about it you know I'm right Tony"

It did make sense what he was saying. I can't base my decision on my relationship with Blane. What if we break up my family would be in Canada i would alone. If i go to Canada i would have my family even a younger sibling and Ian.

I want to go. I will tell Blane. He would understand. We could even have a long distance relationship. I just don't want to loose him.

"We're here" Ian says. He had even opened the car door for me but i didn't notice.

"Thank you" i said as i hugged him.

I held him for a while before i let him go and headed to my own house. I walked in and saw Logan-i mean Papa cuddled up on the sofa watching a movie.

Seeing them together like that gave me some sort of assurance. I wanted my parents, a sibling and a happy family.

"Hello mom?" I greeted.

"Hey sweetheart we didn't hear you come in?"

"I just got here."

"Hey Princess" Logan said

"Hey, how are you guys?"

"We're good. Are you still going with us to the doctor's tomorrow?"

"Wouldn't miss it for the world mom" i kissed he cheek and Logan's nad went up stairs.

I went to my room and sat on my bed and watched friends tolill i fell asleep.

CHAPTER 38: Not just one

We were all having breakfast that Ligan made. He was incredible at cooking he reminded me of Gwen how she said she wanted to become a Chef.

Logan has been handling his business through conference calls since he had someone over there that he trusted.

We all drove in Logan's Range rover i was seated in the back when i got a text from Blane.

Hey Princess X :)

Hey....... Don't call me that Papa calls me that it would be wierd if you both gave me the same pet name... X :)

What do you want me to call you Mi Amor X ;)

That could work ...... just got to the hospital I'll text you later X :)

Hope everything goes well :)

I did feel guilty for not telling him about well everything but I just feel like something is telling me to wait and not tell him yet.

We went into the doctor office and they talked for a while. Then the doctor laid my mother down and spread some jelly on her stomach.

"Ready to find out the gender?" The male doctor asked.

"Yes"

"Looks like a boy" he said but kept his eyes fixed on the monitor.

"And another boy" he finally said.

"What!" My mother immediately asked.

"Your having twins and they are both boys" he said.

"But when we went for a our last check up it was just one baby"

"Sometimes the babies hide behind each other hence the doctor thinks its just one but as you can see on the monitor. There are two babies. Congratulations Mrs. Martinez" he said.

Logan looked very surprised but i could see how happy he still was.

"Thank you Hali, I'm having two boys we can do this together all of us as a family" he said as he also looked at me.

"Congratulations Mom" i said as i let my hand rub her belly.

She was three and a half months pregnant. I couldn't help but think about the family i was soon to have and i didn't want to miss it.

"Have you thought of baby names?" I asked once we were back in the car.

"Yeah if it was a boy Jayden Victoria Martinez and a girl Kayla Victoria Martinez" Logan answered.

I felt tears threating to escape my eyes.

"You gave them my name?" I asked the obvious.

"Yes i did"

I was silent for a while and just looked out the window.

"You know you can change Kayla to Kayden " i said suddenly.

"That's a wonderful idea" my mom answered.

"Jayden and Kayden Victoria Martinez" i said. I let out a loud laugh.

"They are going to hate that you guys gave them a girls name" i said as i imagined the boys arguing with our parents cause of their names.

"They'll just have to deal with it" logan said.

"Thank you" i said.

We drove to a sushi place since Mom started complaining and literally demanding the food.

We were done eating and were sitting waiting for the food to digests we drank for a while.

"I will go with you guys to Canada" i said abruptly.

My parents looked at each other as if they didn't hear me well.

"Don't look at me like that someone has to the fun on in the house" i said

"Are you saying were are boring people people" my dad said with a fake hurt expression.

"We were having fun making the twins and other times" my mom said as she leaned in and kissed Logan.

"Oh my god we are in public and I'm right Infront of me can you guys not!" I said as i held my hand over my eyes.

"I thought you wanted us to be fun" my mom answered as she laughed really loud.

"Whatever mom can we head back home"

"Sure Princess" Logan answered.

I loved seeing my mom like that she was happy care free. Not like when she had to go to work and come home exhausted. I could sometimes hear her cry at night when i went downstairs but she was always strong for me.

She never wanted me to see her being weak and vulnerable. I always wanted to be as strong as her. She was left with a child and the man she loved lived with another woman but she still took care of me.

When we arrived home i wrapped my arms around my mother and hugged her. She waa confused at first bit hugged me back.

"Thank you mom" i said

"For what sweetie"

"Everything being strong for me. And I'm sorry for not understanding at first with Papa" i said.

I looked over at Logan and saw he was surprised i called him Papa instead of Logan.

I pulled away from my mother and hugged Papa.

"Thank you for making her happy again. If you leave again don't think about coming back."

"I'd rather die than leave my family again. I love you so much always have and your mom and Jayden and Kayden"

I smiled into his chest."Thank you for agreeing to come with us to Canada" he said.

My mom came in and hugged both of us making us erupt in a fit of laughter.

"I want pumpkin cake" my mom said.

"That's what you get for having fun Papa" i said as i laughed and went upstairs.

I almost screamed when i saw Ian on my bed with his laptop stuffing his face with chips.

"What the fuck Ian" i shouted

"What"

""Why are you here when no one was home?"

"First you left the window open i thought it was an invitation" he laughed before he continued " second i had a little arguement with mother dearest"

"Was not an invitation and what did you guys argue about?"

"Nothing"

"Come on Ian you just you argued it can't over nothing"

"Its about money. I told her i would go to university with you in Canada. She has no problem with me going its just the costs, the apartment, the food and paying for the fee it's too much" he said then let out a loud sigh

"I'm sorry Ian. I didn't think about all this before dragging you into going with ....." He cut me off

"You never asked me to go with me it was my choice. It's not a problem i will still go with you i can get a student loan or something. "

"No Ian you'll be in debt and have to get a job. If you will have an easier life its better if you stay."

"It's go to sleep it's already late we'll talk about it another time."

He pulled the sheets and pulled me in.

"She is having twins two boys" i said with a smile on my face.

"Just like there uncles" he said referring to him and Ric.

"They are called Jayden and Kayden Victoria Martinez" i said.

"They are so going to hate their middle name" he said with a laugh

"That's exactly what i said"

"Goodnight Tony"

"Night night Iano"

CHAPTER 39: Saint John industries

BLANE'S POV

I hated it whenever my father was around he was always demanding things. Reminding me of how I'm the reason he lost his wife. How it was my fault that my mother was not with me growing up amd i had nannies.

I was a child but he didn't care he left went on trips and never thought about calling or anything. Victoria made me accept my mother's death was not my fault.

Victoria has been the highlight of my life i want her. Everything is okay right now but i feel like it won't last.

"Boy!" I hear my supposed father's voice.

I walk in the living room and he is seated alone on the couch so i sith opposite him.

"Saint John industries will be yours one day "

I nod my head to let him know he should continue.

"When I speak you answer me with your voice Boy!"

"Yes father"

"Good. We all had to make sacrifices for this company even my wife. So will you"

"What kind of sacrifices "

"You are nineteen, you are getting married at 24 ...."

"Father I "

"You don't interrupt me when i talk Boy don't you have any manners. You will apologize and shut up and let me finish"

"I apologize father" looking at him directly.

He stared at me before he continued.

"You will marry Bella and our companies can be one they will own 50 percent of our company and us theirs as well"

"This will be good for our company. Your mother and i worked really hard for it and you are able to save it. You be under me in the company and when you are married and only then will i give you the company"

"Your mother owned Forty five perfect of the company the rest is mine. We might loose everything if this marriage does not happen."

I kept quiet and decided to listen to him. I wouldn't care less if the company was his but he did built it with my mother. She was very proud of the company she built and that's why I'm listening. I don't want my mother's hard work to just get lost, i would do whatever it took to save the company.

I would sacrifice anything to make sure what my mother work to build was lost and if getting married to Bella was the only was then so be it.

"You have to get engaged so that the Collins Company can agree to partner with us."

"But father i thought you and Bella's father were friends can't he just help out?"

"I really hope you stop thinking like a little boy by the time i hand you the company or else the will be lost despite his help"

I kept quiet.

"Collins is a businessman above all else and he thinks like a businessman and this won't just be beneficial to us alone he would benefit alot from this and he also needs a suitor for his daughter and she is interested in you. He decided to kill two birds with one stone."

"I understand father"

"The help he provides would be enough until you get married the company would manage with a few cuts. So Boy what do you say? Do you want to save your mother's hard work?"

"Yes father"

He looked at me and nodded and the he walked out.

I sat and stared at where he had sat. Victoria was the only thing on my mind. I know i have to do this. I don't want Bella to be wife i want Victoria, i want children with Victoria, i want to grow old with Victoria, i want Victoria to take care of me of me when sick not Bella i dont want any of these things with Bella.

"Sweetheart" i heard Cali's voice call me.

"Hey Cali"

She walked and sat next to me. She held my hand and made me look at her.

INSECURE AND CONFIDENT

"Listen to me son, your mother worked hard for the company and she loved it with her life but she loved something else more. She loved you alot more than any company. She wanted the best for you she always talk to you when you were still in her. She wants you to fulfill your dream. If she was here she would do anything to save the company except as you to sacrifice your happiness."

"Did mom want me to marry Bella?"

"Bella's mother was her bestfriend and she hoped their children and maybe get married but she would never force you to do it."

"That was her fantasy apart from the Company"

"Yes. But son your life is your life, not your father's and you alone can decide what to do with it. Only you can choose to marry no one can force you"

"What about Victoria?" I asked

"As i said your life is yours and you do what you want"

"Thank you Cali" i said then hugged her.

She was the closet thing to a parent i had and i loved her.

"I'm always here for you sweetie" i smiled and got up.

I needed to get drunk it seemed like what i ended up doing whenever Adam Saint John was around.

Bella was a year older than i was. I admit there was a time I would have been very happy about marrying her but I'm not.

@@*@*@*

After hours at some fancy bar i went to. I was drunk beyond i couldn't even see my phone. I asked the guy that was serving me to call an uber.

After a few minutes my uber had arrived. I was driven to my house and payed the uber.

I opened my door and went to my room. I feel on the floor in my room.

The room to the door opened and Bella walked in in a thong and nothing on top. She walked towards me and placed me on my bed. She walked to the closet and then walked back towards me. She gave me glass of water and i drank all of it.

She cradled me and her tits were directly in my face. She removed my shirt and he hands roamed all over my chest. Then she kissed me. I tried to resist at first but i for some reason I couldn't like i had no control.

I pulled away and kissed her neck as i held her breasts. I moved as kissed her towards her breasts that were being massaged by my hand. I held her nipple and liked the other on with my tongue and she let out a moan.

I kept on sucking her breasts and i moved my hand to her ass and laid her down. I sucked her other breast and held her other. My free hand was making its way to her clit.

I was feeling like Bella was all i wanted in that moment. I tried to resist my urges but i couldn't.

CHAPTER 39: Father Daughter

Victoria's pov

Since Saturday i haven't seen Blane he just texts me vaguely when i want us to meet up he always comes up with something. Maybe I'm just over thinking things but I can't help but feel like something's very wrong.

We were in a Taxi with Logan i have no idea where we were heading he said it was a surprise. Although i didn't understand why he didn't take his car i decided bot yo ask questions.

"Are you okay Princess?" He asked.

"Yeah I'm okay just thinking"

"Okay. I have two surprises for you i think you'll like the second one more" he smiled at me.

We arrived at a car dealership and a man came towards Logan and they hugged.

"Princess, this is Andreas a good friend of mine"

"Nice to meet you Andreas"

"This is Hali's daughter?" Andreas asked

"Yes she our daughter" Logan answered

"Nice to finally meet you Princess. Follow me Logan"

We gollowed him, i saw alot of acr he must be the owner of the place. He sells cars. Why would Ligan need another car?

We stopped Infront of a cute little beetle convertible car. Then they a turned to me.

"Do you like it Princess?"

"Yeah it's really nice but why are you asking me?"

"Cause Princess its your first surprise" he said smiling widely at me.

"But i don't need a car Ian drives me everywhere i need"

"I know that Princess but you need your own car I thought this would do for the two month we are here. So that you don't have to rely on Ian or Blane all the time"

I mived closer to him amd hugged him.

"Thank you Papa"

"It was no problem Princess."

He gave me the keys then told me the reason we didn't drive his car. He wanted me to drive my new car.

I was excited having my own car. He handed me the keys and we left Andreas car dealership.

I was driving around feeling the new car and the wind.

"Where are we going to now?"

"I'll give directions."

I nodded. We drove to a place he seemed to know well. We stopped Infront of a diner called Nico's.

I looked at my dad questioningly.

"I used to bring Gwen and Coda here whenever i was around its my favourite place to go. They have the best pizzas.

We got out of the car and went into the small diner. It was so homey and welcoming unlike the huge restaurants that make you feel self conscious. The place looked like everyone was welcome.

As I looked around to a place to sit Papa grabbed my hand and led me to a specific booth. When we got to it someone was already there.

His back looed oddly familiar. He turned his face and i could see him.

"Coda!" I screamed making people turn and look at me.

I honestly loved Coda alot and every time i saw him i was happy.

"Hey Victoria " he said as he stood to hug me.

"I missed your unkempt hair" i said into his shoulder.

"I always told his told him to comb that hair" Logan said

"I never got to it Papa" he said with a cheeky smile.

They hugged and laughed. It was nice seeing how Logan had a good relationship with Gwen and Coda.

We sat together in the booth and a waitress came out and took our order.

"So Papa what are you doing here?"

"I introduced you to this place i should ask you that" he said with a chuckle.

"Come on Papa you know its my favourite place to be when i need to think"

"Its mine too. I came to show your sister the best place to get pizza"

"He's not wrong.. Sister"

"What do you need to think about?"i asked

"It's just stuff"

"Coda ...... Spill"

He looked at me then sighed.

"Okay. Its Grandpa" he said looking at Papa.

"He wants me to take ovee the Company so i have to move but i don't want to leave Gwen alone"

"I never liked your Grandpa. He's a pain in the ass" he said making Coda and I laugh.

"I agree. I've always wanted to take over the company but after Gwen's finished high school"

"Its only two months why doesn't he wait then you can go" i said.

"If only he'll listen he's very demanding"

Our food had arrived and Coda was done with his food already.

"I'll leave let you guys have your father daughter day"

"Okay son. And don't forget stand up to your Grandfather he won't do anything to you. Your his favourite" he said laughing.

"Thanks Papa. Bye Little Sister"

"Bye big brother"

He walked out and from the window i could see his car drive off.

Logan amd i ate our pizzas atill we were done making a little chit chat.

"Are you ready for your second surprise?"

"I thought this place was the surprise?"

"No princess it's not"

"I'm ready"

"I know you might have to convince Ian about it but yoyr mother over heard your conversation about the money situation then she told me. I'm sorry if we invaded your privacy"

"It's okay"

"Well i want Ian to live with us together and i will pay for his school as a scholarship and the money he would have used for fees he can use while in Canada as his own however he would like"

"You guys can even move in to an apartment near the school since the estate will be consideringly far from your school. But i will pay for the apartment and your fees both of you and i will give you an allowance every week for your day to day needs. Or if you prefer i can give you one of my cards."

"Why?"i asked

" Because i want you with us in Canada and if i can do anything to make you feel happy while your staying there then i will do it. I know how much

Ian means to you and you to him. He was willing to go with you to a new country. That is loyalty and I'm happy you have someone who i ready to do anything for you at your side."

I felt my tears almost fall from my eyes and i blinked them away immediately.

"Thank you so much Papa. "

"Can i tell you something?" I asked

"Anything Princess"

"A part of me doesn't want to go to Canada"

"Is this cause of your boyfriend"

"Maybe"

"You still aren't sure Princess. Give him time stay with him and enjoy this moment while you have it and when the right time comes you'll know if he is worth it"

"I'm afraid he is it scares me. Not being sure of my future."

"You don't always have to sure of everything Princess. Sometimes just let things take their course."

We got up and left the diner shortly after. It was already dark and we decided to head home. We drove around for a while before heading home.

When we got home and walked to the front door.

"Papa"

"Yes Princess"

"Thank you for the car and Ian. Thank you for an awesome day that I never thought would happen"

He held me.in his arms and whispered in my ear.

"You've always been my pride and joy and you accepting me as your Papa is the best present a father could ever receive, so thank YOU Princess."

"Your welcome Papa"

CHAPTER 40: Beach

Blane's Pov

It's been a two month since i slept with Bella and saying i regret it wouldn't be enough. I betrayed the only person that cared despite what i did.

The only person who didn't care for my inherited wealth. Except Alex and Sam, we still talk he just relocated. Bella has been hanging on my arm ever since saying stupid things like we were meant to be ...... Its fate ..... We were destined for each other ..... Together we can take over the business world ....

She knows nothing of the business world. I've been learning business ever since i was sixteen. Every summer i was working in my father's office as his assistant. He thought seeing him work would help in in future.

I have learned alot from my summer job. One thing i know for sure is that i can do it even better than he is doing it but its not what i want to do.

Victoria and I are still together but everytime i see her my guilt kills me. I want to tell her of but i don't want to loose her. I was drunk and I wasn't thinking. It was as if Bella has been waiting for the perfect opportunity. A vulnerability of sort and she did. She got me right where she wanted me and i stupidly fell for her trap.

Bella decided she would stay in my house and my parents allowed it saying we should bond since we would be married.

Just the thought made me want to disappear. I kept Victoria away from my house all costs afraid Bella might say something. She did come around but when i was sure Bella was not around.

I know Victoria deserves better. I know i have to let her go but I'm scared I'd lose her forever. It's two weeks to graduation this weekend is prom i told Bella I'm not going since she wanted to be my date and i didn't.

Alot has happened in the two months whenever i could i did spend my time with Victoria and tried to make it as memorable as i could.

Flashback

We were at a beach for the weekend it was quite far so we decided to come for the whole weekend and just stay in a hotel she allowed me to pay for our room but on the condition she pays for all the meals and any extras.

We were seated on the beach watching the stars.

"This is so cheesy. Watching the stars the beach" she said with a laugh.

"You know what would be really cheesy?" I asked.

"What could be more cheesy than this"

"We walk in different directions and then start running towards each other in slow motion"

She looked at me as i looked at her. I knew we were thinking the same thing. We both got up and went towards different directions.

"When i get to you i will just then you catch me. Up for the challenge Saint John"

"You know I'm not one to turn down a challenge" i replied from the opposite side.

"Now" she shouted.

She ran towards me slowly and ao did i towards her.

I was savouring the moment knowing that one day I won't have her as my friend much less a girlfriend.

Her hairs that strayed were blowing away as the wind hit her. She was laughing ear to ear amd i wished someone was video taping this moment.

She almost close to me so I got ready to catch her as she jumped.

I nodded for her to jump telling her I'm ready. When she got close enough to jump i caught her. My hands were at her thighs close to her butt. Her hands were around my neck and she stared at me and I her.

"You caught me" she stated.

"I'll always catch you Martinez. Always"

I kissed her immediately and dominated her lips and squeezing her butt which made her gasp hence entrance for my tongue to explore her mouth.

Our lips danced perfectly in synch it all the novels say when you just feel like someone is meant for you amd you alone.

We pulled away for breathe when she jumped down.

"How about we walk along the beach"

"Okay just one minute"

I watched her run to where we had sat and take her phone that waa convincingly placed. She walked to where i was and shut her phone and placed it back in her shorts.

"Did you take a video of us?"I questioned

"Yes. Problem Romeo"

"Why none at all Juliet"

Ww walked along the beach for a while till she decided we should try something.

"What do want us to try?" I asked intrigued.

"We should go for a swim"

"Just that"

"Naked!" She said.

My interest was piqued. I raised my eyebrow at her. I was the one who would propose skinny-dipping but this was all her.

"I think I'm a bad influence Martinez"

"Or maybe I'm the bad influence"

"I'm starting to think you are. Should I be weary of your company "

"We both know you can't stay away" she said as she walked away to get cover as she undressed.

"I'll have to stay away whether i like it or not" i murmured.

"What was that"

"Nothing" i started undressing "race you to the water. Last one is sleeping on the floor"

"You are such a child" she said making me halt and look at her direction.

She walked slowly and suddenly started running towards the water.

I quickly tried to catch up but she was too far ahead. She got in the water laughing.

"Guess i have the bed all to myself" she said.

End of Flashback.

"Babe" Bella called i mentally groaned

"What do you want Bella"

"You better fix your attitude first" she said

"I'm leaving"

"I don't object to you leaving but just know this Blaney bear, if your not nice to me i might talk to my father about how my future might be full of depression and he might disagree to this marriage meaning your company go bye bye" she said adding a sweet smile at the end and leaving.

She infuriated me. How could not see how was before. Victoria tried to but i didn't know.

She wasn't always bad she used to be really nice. Maybe once we are married she'll be how she used to be.

I let out a sigh as i left my house went out to go buy a suit and keep it at Alex's place.

CHAPTER 41: Perfect

Victoria's Pov

The past two months have been the best. Blane and i spent every minute we could spare together. We still studied so that i could maintain my grades up so did he.

Ric came back from his holiday with his girlfriend with a lot of pictures, we Video called together since we were tired of waiting to meet her face to face. She was pretty nice but overly cheery and excited. Guess opposites do attract.

We talked to him about moving to Canada. He said he wasn't surprised with the news cause Ian and I always did almost everything together. He said

"You and Ian are like the white part of the egg and the york. Ian being the white part that will always be there to protect the york which is you."

Ian and laughed at his remark bit deep down we both knew it was true. He was always there shielding me from any sort of harm. I love him to death and i knew he did too.

Ian and I talked about how he felt for me and he seemed to have come to his senses.

I wasn't sure whether to believe him but i took what i could and moved on.

I thanked God for not crossing paths with Bella since she decided to stay at Blane's house for who knows what. Regards Blane and i did have fun.

Flashback

Ian, Ric, Brian and I were walking around the gallery hall looking at the art being displayed. It was charity event that happened every year. Students submit different art and people pay to enter and look and vote for the best art work.

I never attended any but this time i had to well to support my boyfriend who submitted his art. He refused to show me but it was a new one that he painted and refused to show me until today.

We walked aimlessly looking for Blane but nothing so we decided to get drinks. Non alcoholic of course since we were in school.

"You made it" i heard Blane say his mouth dangerously close to my ear.

"And deny myself of your genius. Never." I said as i turned and kissed him lightly on his lips and quickly pulled away.

"Follow me then" he held my hand leading me God knows where but i followed watching myself so that i didn't trip.

He stopped abruptly i almost walked into him but quickly composed myself as i looked up.

It was his paintings. It was definitely a girl with black curly hair. she was in water and water was dripping from her face. It was a side profile, only half a face seen. The girls eyes were bright as she stared at the moonI was zoned out until I heard Ian speak

"Woah he painted her"

I immediately turned to face Blane. Not believing he actually painted me. He nodded and i immediately engulfed him in a hug.

"I think you exaggerated my eyes" i said with a chuckle.

"I don't think so"

"Come on my eyes aren't that beautiful"

He pulled back and held my face in his hands forcing me to look at him he didn't speak for a while as we just stared.

"Your eyes may not be the brightest or prettiest but in my eyes no one could compare to what you have not only your eyes but everything about you Victoria"

"Your perfect Blane. I know you'll never do anything to hurt me. Thank you"

"Thank you for what?"

"You could have any girl but somehow i am your girlfriend so thank you for picking me at least"

"I can assure it wasn't intentional"

"Prick!"

End of Flashback.

Prom was this weekend Blane asked to be his date he didn't do anything frand since i asked him not to.

He took me to dinner and asked like a normal huma being.

We were all in the Smoothie hut after school. It was on a Thursday and Friday's were basically weekends to me.

Brian was talking about his prom tux amd excited would not even begin to explain what he was feeling.

He Always wanted to do something in Fashion hence his excitement of him choose his and his boyfriend's tux.

"Oh my God Vic!" Brian called

"What!" I said immediately ending my train of thought.

"Please don't say no"

"Depends, what you want?"

"Please let me shop for your prom dress?" He was pulling out puppy dog eyes but they didn't work on me except from kids.

Knowing Brian if i allow him it would be such a big deal for him. If he really wanted to who am i to refuse.

"Okay but not anything too much I'll give you my card" i said and he immediately cheered.

I handed him my card and he immediately got up.

"Where are you going?" Ric asked.

"Dress shopping what does it look like. Let's go Alex"

They bid us goodbye and drove off to God knows where to shop. I was honestly happy cause if he I would have had to do last minute shopping since it was one day to prom.

Ian, Ric and i were left in the Hut. I would have asked Cynthia to join us but she apparently quit her job and I've no contact with her whatsoever. I tried calling but it was always disconnected.

"So Ian going all alone to Prom?" Ric asked mockingly at his brother.

I was also curious so i turned my face and looked at him.

"Actually No I'm not. " He answered

"Whoa are you going with?" I immediately asked.

"Gwen!"

"Woah didn't see that coming!" Ric exclaimed

"I mean she is cool and we are going just as friends"

"That's great" i said.

It really was nice, Gwen is super nice when you get to know the good side of her and her and Ian would make an excruciatingly cute couple.

"So we will go to Brian's house to pick him uo then to Alex's place where Blane would be then come pick you girls up at Gwen's" he said. A plan i had no idea about. I didn't know i was going to dress up at Gwen's place.

"I'll ask Gwen to come at my place then you can pick us up there" i said.

I knew my mom would be pissed if i went to prom without her taking pictures and stuff. And i secretly wanted to come down the stairs and see my parents standing there cheering me on about how beautiful i looked.

We left the Hut after twenty minutes and ian and i drove in my car back home while Ric drove his and Ian's car.

We got home and walked to the door.

"See you tomorrow Iano"

"Sleep tight Tony"

He hugged me and kissed my forehead and walked to his house.

I walked inside my house. Dunner was ready Logan cooked as usual.

"I can't believe you almost graduating!"

"I know mom"

The pregnancy was making her very emotional I felt everytime someone said something emotional or cute she was on the verge of tears.

Her belly was huge. She was to deliver her babies in less than four months and i was pretty excited to meet my new brothers, Jayden and Kayden Victoria Martinez.

My phone buzzed..

Goodnight babe . X Your boyfriend.

Sleep well Saint John. X Your girlfriend.

CHAPTER 42: Never been my mother

∧ ^^^^^ A picture of Karen Williams^^^^

I was in the Cafeteria with Ian, Ric and Gwen.

"Where is Brian" i asked directed to no one in particular.

"He faked being sick and was sent home" Ian said

One of Brian's many talents he would make a brilliant actor if he wanted to he could do something and you wouldn't even doubt him cause it was always so believable. His love of Fashion over powered theater as he said.

"Ian your suit should be plain black" Gwen demanded.

"Why?"

"Cause I'm wearing gold and i want us to match plus black makes you look sexy" she said.

I fake gagged "SpongeBob would be sexier in a black suit than this Dumbass" I said making Ric and i laugh loudly.

"Okay Gwen I'll wear a full black suitSome people just can't accept how irresistible i am" he said looking directly at me with a glint of playfulness.

My phone buzzed

Meet me in the hallway of room 215. X Blane.

On my way. X Victoria

"Gotta go" i said immediately after reading the text.

"Your driving home with me yeah?" Gwen said.

"Yap"

We were going to her place for a sleepover so that we would do what we needed together morning then head to my place in the afternoon to get dressed for Prom.

The hallway was a little bit far form the cafeteria area , i got there in 5 minutes.

I saw Blane leaning on the wall and i walked towards him.

Immediately i got to him he dragged me into the room that was nearby.

He closed the door and pushed me against it placing his lips on mine. I was flustered at first but immediately regained my composure and kissed him back with equal amount of excitement.

He slowly lead me to the table and placed me on top. We separated for air bit he continued his assault on my neck i let my hand run through his hair as he sucked on one specific spot.

He was marking me but i didn't mind so let him. When he was satisfied with his work he kissed the spot and came back to my lips, when the door suddenly burst open making me pull away from Blane.

I looked at the boy in glasses holding a few books. When he noticed Blane he muttered a series of sorrys as he quickly left the room closing the door behind him.

I had forgotten how most kids in school in school weren't fond of Blane cause he usually was with the jocks or alone and not very approachable.

"You need to stop being so scary?" I said as he looked at me.

"It's not my fault?" He said with a shrug

"So threating to have a teacher fired for giving you an A and beating up a kid for saying something you didn't like and lets not forget your father literally...."

"Okay okay i get it but Mrs. Green graded my paper unfairly it was on point and the kid called Alex a fag how was i not to react?"

"Okay the kid did deserve it" i said.

I was still on top of the table and he was holding my waist.

I wanted my prom night to be special and i know its so cliché but i wanted to sleep with Blane. He has never asked me about it he has always know i wasn't ready but now i think I am.

"Should I tell you something?"

"Anything?"

"I think we should go to a hotel or something after prom and spend the night just the two of us" i said as i looked at my hands.

He held my face and lifted my face and i could see the realisation of what i just said in his eyes.

"Are you sure?" He asked i could see something in his eyes i could see his feelings for me but the guilt in his eyes was so kuch stronger.

Why was he feeling guilty? I asked myself. After a few seconds my mind told me maybe it cause he thought he was forcing me into it.

"Yes I'm sure unless your not?"

"It's not that Victoria"

"So you'll do the booking" i said amd he just nodded. Immediately the bell rang we had to go our separate ways since we didn't have the same class.

.....

We were in the parking lot and i was going to go with Gwen straight to her place.

"I'll see you tomorrow?" Blane said pulling me towards him.

"I am your date after all"

I leaned in and kissed him i was slowly beginning to forget we were around people well until

"Come on guys your going to make me throw up my lunch!" He said with fake gags and we pulled away.

"Until tomorrow Martinez"

"See you then Saint John"

I got in the car with Gwen and we drove away.

.

"So you and Ian?" I asked wriggling my brows.

She laughed and said "we are going just as friends plus we probably won't see eachother for i don't know how long?"

She knew that after graduation we were leaving sge was supportive but made me promise not to forget to text her or call her and i plan on keeping that promise.

Gwen had become more than i would want in a sister she was incredible as a friend and just perfect as a sister even a just step sister.

We walked into their huge Manor and headed to the living room. I saw Coda sitting and an older woman bit still very beautiful.

I looked at Gwen and saw her look at the woman any trace of happiness in her face was no longer there.

"What the fuck is she doing here Coda?" She said in a very low and dangerous voice.

Gwen has been mad with her parents she told me but hated her mother. She was a "selfish woman who only cares about herself and i don't blame Dad for leaving her" her words exactly.

She forgave Logan cause aa she said "at least he called us from time to time and we would talk for long amd he genuinely cared about his children and if he did fall in love with another woman it wasn't his fault and I can't blame him. I know he loves Coda and I can't say the same for mother dearest"

"Did you really think i would miss your graduation Gwen?" Karen, her mother said.

"You missed everything so far except for my birth and that's cause you couldn't escape that so again why are you here?" Gwen retorted quickly losing patience.

"Don't you think we can discuss this later now you can introduce me to your friend?" She said looking at me with a not so friendly face.

"Mom this is Victoria Martinez" Coda answered.

I could see the wheels in her head turn.

"What is this Bastard doing in my house?" She shouted at me

"You mean our step sister than we love she is just sleeping over do you have a problem?" Gwen quickly said not giving me an opportunity to answer.

"Love? You love this g- girl she was a result of what made this family grow apart Son can you put some sense into your sister?"

"I don't think she was the reason our family apart mother" Coda said in a very calm voice making everyone surprised.

Coda was always a mother's boy he would always support her no matter what. I could see Karen visibly surprised even Gwen couldn't believe it. Even i didn't except him to say that.

"What!" She said looking at Coda

"She is not the reason our father left that was all you and your selfish ways. You couldn't let him take care of his children not just Victoria even Gwen and I. When you got Dad back what did you do you told him to leave with you alone not thinking about us. Leaving us in the care of nannies. Even in the holidays he forced you to come see you own Children."

"You know I once blamed Dad for cheating bit he still took care of us but you! I had to take care of you i was barely four years old when you started doing drugs and you didn't care if i ate or not. You never let me be a kid!" Coda finished his outburst looking like he was on the verge of tears.

He seemed to have kept his feelings in for so long.

"I think the damaged you've already caused since we were children is enough we would feel better if you left and this house is not yours it Grandfather's and it's in Coda's name its his house not yours and right now I don't think the owner of the house wants you here Karen!" Gwen said looking at her mother dead in the eye.

"Your really kicking me out cause of her! Her mother ruined my life!" She shouted.

I felt guilty cause my mom did ruin her marriage but her relationship with her kids is all her.

"That Woman! Her mother! Hali has been more of a mother the last few months than you would ever be in a lifetime. She genuinely wanted to talk and know us even though we are not her children she made us know a mother's love. You everything coming her way and you will be alone not a husband that you so desperately wanted and not the children you didn't care about. YOU HAVE NEVER BEEN MY MOTHER.Please Get Out!" Gwen so strongly responded.

It was true my mother really loved Gwen ans Coda we've been spending every Sunday together even when i wasn't there for some Sundays they still spent time together and my mom loved Coda and Gwen.

Some would be jealous cause of all tge attention they got but I didn't care i had her all to myself for more than ten years and sharing her right now was okay for me.

I didn't get all the attention from Logan which is a plus.

I walked to where Coda was standing. I could see that he was bottling up all the feelings about his Mother. I held him and pulled her in for a hug.

I heard his sobs as i hugged him even more tightly.

"Your very strong Coda. You've been strong for so long" i said.

At the corner of my eyes i could see Karen drag her stiff and leave the house.

Gwen came and joined in the hug and i could see she was also crying. I held both of the tightly as i remained silent and ket them cool off.

****

Ps. Longest chapter I've ever written

****

CHAPTER 43: I'll see you soon

"For the love of God wake up already!" Gwen frustratedly said.

I groaned again. She's been trying to wake me up for the last half hour. But in my defence we slept pretty late last night.

After Karen left yesterday day and Coda cooled down and decided alcohol was the solution, we stayed up for the next five hours or so. We went to bed at 1 am.

She wanted me to wake up at 8. My body and my brain didn't agree. But God her voice was annoying when she kept on repeating the same thing 'wake up'.

"I swear if you don't get up i throwing water on you!"

As much as I really wanted to keep on sleeping i didn't want to be drenched in water more. I got up not saying a word went into the bathroom and shutting the door.

I washed up, brushed my teeth and got out half expecting Gwen to be gone but I wasn't that lucky today.

"Goodmorning Gwen" i said as i went to my bag and pulled out a shirt and a pair of shorts cause it really hot. Gwen was also already dressed in very short shorts and a crop top that showed a generous amount of cleavage and not too far past her breasts.

She looked nice but it's not something i would be comfortable in.

"First we have massages then manicure and pedicures. Then i have to body waxed you can too i booked yours too if you want. Then we have to go pick up my necklace from the jeweler. I already have my two dresses which again you have yo help me decide which is better. We have so much to do and you didn't want ....."

"Woah hold up" i interrupted cause she was fast rambling i didn't get most of what she said.

"How about we start with food first, you know the most important meal of the day?" I finished making her groan and waving me to follow her.

I can smell the delicious food from the door. Bacon, eggs and toast and plate with slices of oranges and a banana.

"I want to hire you as my personal chef!" I said as i moaned as i ate every bite.

"You wouldn't be able to afford me and I don't want to be anyone's servant" she retorted.

She cooked the bacon to perfection not burnt in the slightest unlike my mom's. Which reminded me i needed to call my mom.

Immediately i was done eating and cleaned the dishes i called my mom asking how she was and telling i was good then she asked to speak to Gwen. And they were still talking.

"I thought we had a load shit of stuff to do!" I said reminding her of the reason she woke me up so early on a Saturday.

She said bye to my mom and prepared food for Coda and left it for when he would wake up.

She carried her two dresses and placed them perfectly on the back of the car mad my stuff.

My phone rang and i immediately picked it up not checking the caller ID.

"Hello"

"Goodmorning beautiful" on queue i knew who it was.

"Goodmorning handsome"

"What are you up to?"

"Gwen is dragging around town to do stuff then later drive to my place"

"I knew it, you wouldn't volunteringly wake up before 10 on a Saturday"

"Are you calling me lazy Saint John. I can't believe you a girl decides to sleep on one day a week all of a sudden she is lazy.."

"What will you do about it?" Definitely not the reaction i was hoping for.

"A normal boyfriend would get worried about making her girlfriend mad but you don ..."

"First i am everything BUT normal plus i know you can't get mad at me for being utterly truthful" i could see the smirk on his face.

"Can you guys stop being so cute God. Your going to make me puke!" Gwen said very loudly so that Blane could also hear.

"Bye babe. Don't want to upset the big scary Witch!"

"See you later!" I say as i hung up the phone.

We arrived at the heart of the city and headed toward the massages first. Gwen didn't spare any expense at getting the best massages we could get. I felt like i could do anything after i got out of there.

We went to the next saloon for our nails. Gwen was sure about her dress colour being gold ao she got gold nails. I wasn't sure about my dress but i knew by the time i got home it would be in my room waiting. So i got black with glitter.

After the nails that matched our toe nails we went to get waxed. Gwen was used to it already bit he wasn't it was my first time i only agreed to it cause of what i would happen after prom. It was painful but managed to handle it and not run out.

We were heading to the jewelry store for Gwen's necklace. This wasn't just prom to her as she said 'every event is important even as small as school dances and we have to take them seriously that's why I'm going through all this for a stupid prom night. I'm practicing for my future and all the events my name will drag me too'

Being a WILLIAMS did have responsibility. it was famous name and with Coda she would get dragged to alot so i was cool with her being all crazy.

She got her very expensive necklace when i heard the price i knew she wouldn't buy it cause it was very expensive but alas she did leaving me gawking at her.

She bought a snake type necklace it was really nice and she said it matched her shoes which also had the snake thing.

After all the walking i was exhausted and very hungry. We walked into a restaurant close to the mall.

When we walked in and sat down and ordered our food. I ordered steak cause why not and Gwen ordered a salad saying she didn't want any extra fat on her tonight.

I didn't care. I did want my dress to fit well but not at the expense of my food. Our food arrived and i ordered cold water to go with it.

"By the way Vic when are you going to tell Blane?" Gwen asks

"Tell him what?" I said taking a bite of my meat.

"You know how you plan on literally going to a whole other country?"

"Oh that it's just Canada I still have a week i wi..."

"Victoria" i heard a very annoying voice making me lift my head and look at the the person who so easily distracted me from my food.

Bella.

In all her snobby glory. I plastered a smile on my face and decided to care of this like an intelligent Woman i am.

"Hy bella, this is my step sister, Gwen" i said introducing Bella.

Bella looked at Gwen and smiled. Fake. Gwen glared at her and quickly went back to her salad.

"So Victoria, i your school's prom is today who are you going with?" She asked

"She's going with her boyfriend, of course. Are you someone's date?" Gwen interjected

I saw the anger flash in her eyes but she quickly made it disappear as it came. Then she turned to Gwen.

"Uh no i was just asking. I'll see soon Victoria" with that she walked away incredibly fast and walked out of the restaurant.

"That was Bella the one i told you about. Who lives with Blane" i said to Gwen.

"Woah she's hot and her red hair adds to it. I wonder how Blane hasn't fucked her yet living in the same room?" She said as she went back to her food.

It got me thinking. How long could he go without giving in. I decided to push those thoughts away not wanting to think of the possibility.

We are done eating and i decided to pat for the food. Did i mention Logan gave a credit card and it didn't have a limit i could use it however i want.

But i didn't buy any extravagant things mostly food and maybe i shirt or clothing i liked that's it.

We went to her car and she put her stuff in the trunk and we drove to my house.

"We're here!" I shouted as soon as i got in the house and my mom quickly came down the stairs well as fast as she could.

****

Gwen's necklace.....

CHAPTER 44: Anywhere but home

B lane's Pov (from Friday after school when he left to go home)

I hated going back home to see Bella in my house. I dreaded going back to my house i felt like it was infested.

Everytime i saw her I kept on remembering what i did. One thing was on always on mind how could i do that to Vic. Saying the guilt was eating my inside would be an understatement.

I know i should tell her but i really don't want to loose her at least not while we atill have a week to graduation. I will tell her I'm just looking for the right moment. That's what everyone says. I know.

Vic and i haven't talked about us after graduation I haven't mentioned it and she hasn't too. It like we both don't want to talk or even think about it.

I got home and went in the house taking in a deep breath before opening the door.

I went straight to the refrigerator to get a cold drink. When i turned my mood turned more sour as i say her stand at the door way in a crop top and panties.

It was new mode of dressing saying it was too hot to cover up too much.

I walked past her and went to the living room and switched on the tv. I pressed on FRIENDS the series that Victoria loved and she would laugh alot watching i didn't find it as hilarious but it was interesting i especially liked Chandler and Phoebe, i don't have any specific reason as to why i liked those specific characters.

As i watched the series i felt Bella sit next to me in very close proximity. He moved her hand and brushed my hair with her fingers but i stayed focused on what i was doing as paying no mind to her antics.

"Why are you ignoring me Blaney bear?"

There she goes again with the stupid nick name that i oh so much hated.

"I'm not ignoring you I'm just watching something!" I answered

She took the remote and switched the tv off. I felt my blood boil i was fuming but i couldn't do anything to her.

"You should go to prom tomorrow with Me!"

Oh I'm going to prom just not with you. I thought to myself

"I told you I'm not going to some dance I'll be hanging out with Alex and I'm changing my mind. I'm going to bed!" I said as i got up and stormed to my room. I know it sounds childish bit God ahe gets on my last nerve.

I obviously wasn't going to sleep it was just 8pm and too early. I switched on the Television in my room and decided to play video games.

After a few hours I got tired and slept.

......

"Alex I'm here!" I shout as i walk in his house he alone not far from his parents house that's why i just walked in and did whatever i wanted.

I left early cause my house was obviously no longer one of my favourite places to hang out. She wasn't awake yet so no unnecessary drama for me and i was pretty excited to see my girlfriend in her prom dress when we picked them up.

I walked into living room from the kitchen which was my first stop.

"My God! Get a room!" I say when i see Brian on Alex fully clothed thank God.

"My house i get to do what i want anywhere!" Alex said as he and Brian got off eachother.

We decided to play some video games to pass the time just me and Alex.

Brian has to leave to take Victoria's dress to her house before she got home and he didn't allow me to see it. I had grown fond of Brian he's cool amd we get along well. I get along with all of Vic's friends except Ian.

Ian has a problem with me from day one and i was cool with him until he said he was in love with Victoria then i just flat out hated him. But he was Vic's best friend so i had to tolerate him which i could do as long as he doesn't talk to me and me to him.

After a a few hours of games and a little drinks nothing serious just fun. Brian came back with Ian and his brother Ric who was really quiet but i liked how quiet he was.

"Hey Man are you okay?" Alex asks me out of nowhere.

"Ye yeah why?"

"Just I noticed how you've been deep in thought alot lately just wanted to make sure your all good!"

He knew about me getting married to Bella in a few years and he understood it was what i had to do.

"Can i tell you something?"

"Yes of course!"

"Come with me" i walked of the house and led him to a far distance so that no one would accidentally over hear.

"I cheated on Victoria!" I blurt out.

I felt a little relieved but the guilt seemed to intensify when i finally said it out loud.

"What!"

"I said i cheated on Victoria with Bella two months ago! God!" I said frustratedly as i ran my fingers through my hair.

"How? Why?"

"Trust me it wasn't intentional and I'm proud of it. I was drunk very drunk and when i got home she came to my room naked and gave something to drink water i think and she was naked the only thing on her body was a thong. For some fucked up reason i couldn't stop it's like i wanted her even though I didn't!" I said quickly explaining to my bestfriend.

"Woah that's fucked up man! Does she know?"

"What do you think Alex!" He was silent for a moment and finally spoke

"You know you have to tell her right?"

"I know but God how can i break her heart like that!"

"Guess you'll just have to man up!" He said giving an encouraging tap on the shoulder.

"I'll tell her just not today it can't be today!"

"Okay! Let's go get ready then and make tonight the best night of her life!"

"I intend to!" I said as we walked back to his house.

Honestly i was relieved to atleast tell Alex cause I knew i could trust.

Later on.....

"Okay boys time to get ready we have thirty minutes to get ready the Limo is already here so up up!" Brian obviously said making Ian, Alex and I groan.

We got up and got ready everyone brought their tuxedos with them .

I was in a full black tuxedo so was Ian. Ric was wearing dark blue suit.

We were all sitting waiting for Alex amd Brian till i got really tired.

"Alex and Brian get down here before i drag you to the car!" I shouted from the bottom of the stairway.

Minutes later they both came down Brian was in a white coat and Alex Black. They looked together like they belonged and Alex was very happy with him making me happy for him.

(A picture of Alex amd Brian above ^^^)

"Oh Blane almost forgot i got you this Bow tie that matchs Victoria's dress here" Brian said handing it to me.

It was red meaning she was wearing red! I couldn't wait to see how she looked like in her dress!

We got in the car and told driver our destination, my girlfriend's house.

CHAPTER 45: Prom night

Victoria's Pov

It took two hours to get ready if you ask me that's alot of time but Gwen said we finished faster than she thought.

We were dressed and the boys texted us saying they are on their way and Gwen perfecting her look as she said.

When she deamed herself ready and turned to me i almost groaned knowing she wanted to 'perfect' mine too.

I thought i looked extremely well like beautiful model well.

She made me sit as she perfected my look and smiled as she admired her work my mom was on the bed looking at her girls get ready.

I looked at her and saw a few tears escape her eyes. I quickly got up and sat by her side and wiped the tears away with my thumb. This is the second time she's crying since we arrived home.

"Mom you have to stop crying!" I said as Gwen sat on ger other side holding her hand.

"I can't help it you've grown up so much and it's prom now then graduation in a week then you finish college then you move out then your engaged and then you get married and you don't need me anymore and have children of your own and I'm the Grandma you only talk to during mother's day and my birthday ..." She was full on crying now as she poured her heart out.

"Oh Mama, i think your fast forwarding my life, we have a lot of time together before. I will always be your daughter like it or not even when i have children. And don't forget you'll have two boys to keep you company!" I said as i held her belly.

She looked down and smiled at her two growing boys.

"What about you Gwen when we leave for Canada will you forget all about me cause your also my daughter and don't want yo loose you and Coda?" She asks looking at Gwen.

"Oh you'll to do more than move to Canada to loose ties with us. Your my mother even though not birth i won't let a little distance break what we have plus we be there for holidays!" She says making my mom laugh a little.

Suddenly the door opens and Logan walks in.

"She's crying again!" he says

"See even your father is already tired of me!" She says angrily as she got up and walks past Papa making his eyes grow wide

"Mi amor you know that's not what I meant!" He says as he walks after her.

Gwen amd I looked at each other and laughed at my mom being overly sensitive.

"I hope my pregnancy hormones aren't like that!" She says making me laugh.

"I love your dress Victoria I'll have to make Brian buy all my dresses from now own!" She says after a while

I was wearing a Red off-shoulder dress that Brian bought and altered a little to make look more sexy but modest, hence making my cleavage more visible and cutting off the sleeves.

(Victoria's dress ^^)

"I love your dress the colour makes you look vibrant and incredibly sexy" i tell her .

She was wearing a gold dress that had a slit and showed a long legs and a generous amount of cleavage. She did look amazing and it looked nice with her necklace.

I was excited to see Blane tonight. I was more excited for after the prom when i finally lost my virginity. I don't care if its cliché to loose your virginity on prom night but tonight just feels right.

I know i made Blane wait for so six months but i didn't feel ready. I know other people loosing your virginity is overrated but i don't care it's a big deal for me.

I was pulled out of my thoughts when my dad came in and said the boys where down stairs. I walked into the bathroom cause i suddenly felt nervous i closed the door behind me as i left Gwen and Papa talking.

I looked at myself she mirror and thought about how my senior year has brought alot of things my boyfriend, father, a sister, a brother and two others on the way.

I remembered Frank he had to leave for Germany with his mom but we did talk frequently he was doing great even had a girlfriend of mixed race and incredibly beautiful. I did miss him though.

When i finally felt ready i walked out and saw Papa sitting on the bed.

"Hey" i said as i walked towards him.

"Hey Princess, how you feeling?" He asks smiling at me.

"Pretty nervous!"

"It's happens!" He simply says with a chuckle and just stares at me.

"Why are you just looking at me?" I ask

"Your just so grown up and I missed most of it and it's all my fault. But at least i get to see you and be a part of your life now. I love you so much Princess!" He says as he held me and hugged me.

"I love you too Papa and I'm happy your a part of my life too!"

He held me for a minute longer before pulling away.

"I got this for you i know you'll wear the necklace Blane gave you so i got you a Bracelet so that you can also have something from me." He says as he opened a small box revealing a bracelet covered in diamonds.

"Papa this must cost alot!" I say as i looked at the expensive bracelet.

"You seem to forget I'm a Millionaire Princess" he says with a chuckle making me smile.

"Thank you Papa!" I say and he placed the bracelet on my wrist.

"Logan leave the girl alone or she'll be late!" My mother shouts from downstairs.

"We better go down there before she turns into the evil queen!" Papa says as we both laughed.

We descended the stairs as he held my hand.

Blane was at the bottom looking as handsome as ever in a black tuxedo. He looked so exquisite. He should always wear suits i thought.

He raised his head instantly meeting my eyes. We looked as in we were in our own movie as we looked at each other forgetting everything.

When i got the last stair case he immediately walked towards me and stopped very close to my face.

"Your beautiful!" He says as he looked at me making my breathe hitch.

He held my waist and pulled me in for a kiss which i gladly complaied and kissed him back. We were lost in the kiss well till Papa cleared his throat making the guys laugh aa we pulled away.

"Hey!" I say to Blane but i comes in a whisper.

"Hey" he says back.

"Your handsome!" I say and she laughs making him look more gorgeous.

I quickly snap out of my trance and say hello to the rest of the guys.

"This dress is Gorgeous. Thank you!" I say to Brian

"I knew the dress would look good but damn you gave it life!" He says as his eyes mived across the dress.

"You are beautiful Victoria!" Ian says as he hugged me

"Well Mr. Sexy in black you look very nice too!" I say and he flashed me his award winning smile.

We left after my mom took many pictures and saying we should be careful and be safe she says to Blane specially for some reason.

We were in the Limo everyone talking and just laughing at stuff as we drove to school which wasn't far.

We arrived and Brian and Alex walked together. Gwen intertwined her hand in Ian's. I was obviously walking beside Blane.

"Eric!" Someone shouts out of nowhere making all of us turn.

"Eva?" Ric said as a blonde girl approached him and kissed him.

"I hope you like my surprise!" She says excitedly.

"I love your surprise" he says as he holds her tiny waist.

"Didn't think I'd missed your senior did you? Omg did you ask someone else?" She says suddenly growing mad.

It was very fun seeing the events unfold

"No I would never you know that!" That seems to please the girlfriend and they suddenly remember our presence.

Although we all talked to her on face time Ric formally introduced each of us.

After the introductions we finally went into the school and went into the hall where it was decorated in a ball room fashion but with a DJ. It looked pretty cool.

We found seats and all sat together. We all talked and laughed at some people who already wanted to jump on their dates.

After while we decided to dance and we all went to the dance floor. I wasn't much of a dancer like Gwen and Eva so i was just hyping them up as they danced and Brian and Alex also danced very well.

Ric and watched and cheered as the reat danced even Blane. After a while of just having an awesome time the Principal went on stage and we all knew it was time for Prom King and queen announcement.

" .... And the Prom King is Ian August.." well that was a surprise and everyone turned to look at him. I guess no one guessed that.

Suddenly Brian cheered loudly and everyone followed as Ian walked to take his crown. As Prom King he was to speak.

"Uh This was unexpected but Thank you all very much i am honoured to be a king to loyal servants" he said and everyone burst into laughter even Blane.

"... The Prom Queen is Gwen Williams!" The principal announced. Everybody cheered and she went and gracefully accepted her crown.

"Uh This was expected. Thank you all for choosing me as your Queen." She said shortly and everyone laughed when she said it was expected.

After they did the stupid first royal dance as my school calls it we all went and sat down at the table we were at.

"So how does it feel to be in the presence of royalty you peasants!" Ian said as he laughed.

After a while of drinking punch with a little bit of alcohol Blane asked me to dance it was a slow song playing so i could manage that.

We got to the dance floor and intertwined our fingers as his hand came around my waist and my hand was around his neck and i rested my head on his chest as we slow danced.

"Can I tell you something?" I said suddenly

"Yeah" he answered

"I love you!" I said as the music came to an end and i lifted my head to look at him.

I just said I loved him. I looked at him i could feel he loved me too but he didn't say anything. He just looked at me suddenly i saw guilt in his eyes. He didn't love me back! I panicked

"I need to use the bathroom" i said suddenly as i walked away he called after me but i just kept on walking till i found a bathroom.

I thanked God he didn't follow me.

I stood in the bathroom as i looked at myself in the mirror. I could feel the tears want to escape but I didn't let them.

It wasn't a must for him to love me!

But i hurt that he didn't at least i knew he liked me! Right.

After staying a whole twenty minutes in the bathroom i decided i needed to go bavk out and act like i didn't say anything.

When i was about to walk out someone opened the door and walked in.

"Bella?" I said as she stood Infront of me.

"I told you I'll see you soon" she says with a smirk on her face.

"What do you want?" I asked seemingly bored of her.

"What's wrong Victoria? You seem disappointed or is heart broken?" She said her smirk growing.

She heard me! When i said i loved him and he didn't reply.

"No!" I said not letting her see how Blane's silence affected me.

"Well then your about to be!" She says her smirk and amusement very prominent.

"What are you talking about Bella?" I ask growing irritated.

"I'd rather show you don't you think?" She says as she handed me her phone.

I took her phone and saw it was a video so i pressed play.

I watched the video from beginning. The video started as she was placing a Camera and grabbed a glass and walked to someone on the bed.

I looked closely to see the person on the bed.

BLANE!

He was on his bed and took the glass and drunk it then it was places aside and Bella who was practically naked sat on his lap!

As i watched the more my heart broke. I saw him do things to her kiss her! Touch her cunt! Suck her breasts!

I couldn't stop watching! My eyes were growing watery! The video stopped as he started fucking her!

"When?" Was all that i said as i looked at the black screen.

"Two months ago!" She says with a triumphant look on her face.

I walked past her after handing her her phone.

I walked and got out of the school property. I had my phone so i called Papa to pick me as tears streamed my eyes.

I felt defeated.

I felt lost.

I felt betrayed for two months.

After walking for God knows how long Logan's car stopped Infront of me and i got in and didn't say a word.

CHAPTER 46: I Promise

I didn't sleep. I couldn't.

I felt empty.

I literally didn't feel anything for hours i sat in the same position in my bed and stared at a wall.

Flashes of the video kept on appearing Infront of me.

I was holding on to the necklace he gave me when he asked me to be his girlfriend.

The tears had stopped but i knew if i saw him i wouldn't be able to stop myself from breaking down completely Infront of him.

Was that why he couldn't say he loved me back? Cause he loved Bella all this time ?

Of course he was who wouldn't fall for Ms.. pretty face?

God! Was everything some sick Joke?

I don't want to face him. I couldn't he already took me for a fool!

I heard a knock on the door and quickly wiped my tears away.

Papa walked in and i could see the pity in his eyes but I didn't mind.

"Hey Princess, Ian called and i told him you're okay" i nodded and looked at him.

"Is there anything I can do to make you feel better?" He asked his voice filled with concern.

"Can we leave?"

"Sure Princess where to?"

"Canada" i said blankly.

"But you have graduation next week?"

"Please Papa make something up i was sick anything just please let's go mom amd Ian can come after graduation. Please Papa!" I pleaded as my tears became prominent in my eyes.

"Okay Princess I'll go talk to mom and book the next flight to Canada but you have to sleep amd I'll wake you up two hours before the flight Okay Princess!" He was talking me as you would a little fragile child.

"Okay Papa" i said and he smiled and walked to the door.

As soon as he was out i closed my eyes sleep immediately took me.

......

"Wake up sweetie" i heard my mom's voice as i tried to open my eyes.

When i finally willed my eyes open i looked at the time from the clock beside my bed.

12:34

"Hey honey"

"Hy mom" i answered as i sat up and looked at her.

"I talked to Logan, he told me you want to leave today?" She asked looking concerned.

"Uh yeah!" I said blankly.

"Why?" Ahe asked making me think about everything all over again everything just rushing back to my mind every glory detail.

"I- I'm not ready to take about it Mom just please let me go" i said as my eyes watered making my vision blurry.

She immediately engulfed me in a hug but I didn't want to cry. A few tears slipped but that was it.

"It's okay sweetie. I wasn't going to stop you from going i even packed a bag while you were asleep. The flight leaves at 14:50 you'll go with Logan and I'll follow later. Is that okay sweetie?"

I nodded and she smiled at me getting up leaving me to get ready since we had to arrive early and we still had to drive.

I took a shower quickly and added some stuff in my bag before going downstairs for food.

Papa had already prepared food for me and handed me a plate.

"Here's your phone you left it in the car" he passed me the phone seeing it was fully charged with 20 missed calls and 12 messages.

Vic why aren't you back from the bathroom - Ian

I just checked the and your not there where the hell are you- Ian

We are looking all over for you please text us back- Ric

Vic where are you?- Gwen

Victoria- Ian

God just text me back or answer the damn phone.- Ian

Are you okay?- Brian

We are all worried?- Brian

Your dad said your safe with him but don't make me have HBP at such a young age- Ian

I hope your okay??- Ric

I just saw Bella is that why you left?- Gwen

Blanc just ran out like a crazy person. Is everything okay?- Gwen

I read all the texts making me feel guilty for not telling anyone I left and making them worried but I just didn't think at tge moment.

I'm okay guys sorry for making you worried i just had to leave.- Victoria

I sent that to the group chat we created.

Ian I'm sorry i just up and left without telling you. I had to. I'm leaving to Canada in a an hour you'll come with mom. I'm really sorry.- Victoria

I sent the message to just Ian.

"Princess we have to get going?" Papa said.

I went to my room to take my bag. I looked around the room i grew up in. Where i had my first kiss with Ian, uncountable sleepovers with the boys. The memories i had made me smile even slightly but quickly remembered i had to leave.

"Will you be okay for a week alone?" Papa asked my mother making me again feel guilty.

"It's just a week I'm not completely hopeless you know. Go take care of our Babygirl" my mom said as i got to the last stair case.

They hugged and kissed making me make my way to place my bag in the car.

After Papa and Mom were done with their farewell my mom walked to where i was.

"I'll miss you sweetie" she said

"It's just a week?" I said

"Way too long without seeing your or Logan?"

She hugged me and i hugged her back.

After a few minutes i was getting in the car when i saw Ian's car speeding to our direction.

The car stopped and out came Ian, Ric and Brian.

They all came to where i was.

"What did you think we'd let you leave just like that?" Ian asked.

"How?"

"We were all in the same hotel when Ian got your text and all literally speed up here" Ric said

"What about Alex, Gwen and Eva?"

"Gwen will see you at the airport that's what she said, Eva is still asleep and Alex had to leave " Brian quickly answered.

"Wanna drive me to the airport?" I asked and they quickly nodded.

Logan got in his car after waving bye to my mom and drove off Ian following behind in his car.

No one asked me about last night we just had light conversation until..

"Ian fucked Gwen last night!" Brian as if he just remembered some very important information.

I saw Ian tense next to me making me chuckle a little.

Brian started making exaggerated sex noises making all of us die of laughter and Ian turning red.

"How the hell did you even know!" Ian asked

"Man the whole hotel knew!" He said adding moaning Voices.

For a moment i forgot about everything about Him as we laughed.

He didn't text me.

He didn't call.

He didn't try to explain.

I didn't know if that was a good thing or not i was having an internal battle.

Soon we arrived at the airport and we all got out and walked towards my dad.

I let out a shaky breathe.

I was nervous but what could I do. I would leave eventually so why not now.

I was moving on from a person who cheated on me but also loved way before he even asked me to be his girlfriend.

We walked towards to check in area amd we stopped to say our final good-byes.

I turned and looked at all of them. I hugged Brian as tears started to fkow freely from my eyes when I moved away and he kissed my forehead.

"I'll miss you Vic!"

"Me too Brian " i said as i wiped the teras from my cheeks and hugging Ric next.

"Make more friends when you get to University" i said sternly into his ear

"And have fun!" I added.

"I'll try my best" he said as he chuckled pulling away from the hug.

"Victoria!" I heard Gwen's voice making me turn. I saw her and Coda approach very quickly and immediately hugged me.

"I just got you and your leaving?" Gwen said.

"You'll be over every holiday and call me everyday" i said as i hugged her tightly.

We pulled away and i smiled then whispered in her ear "the boys told me the whoke hotel heard you last night" she blushed turning very red and looking away and talked to Papa.

"Coda!" I said as i literally jumped on him and he caught me.

"I'll miss you too Little Sister!" He said close to my ear.

"I know. I will too Big brother."

After talking for five minutes Papa said we had to check in.

I moved to Ian.

"I'll be waiting for you in a week!" I said as i hugged him.

"See you in a week" he said as he kissed me temple.

Papa and I walked and turned to wave our final good-bye.

After we were settled on the plane seeing he booked first class tickets he looked at me and held my hand amd asked "what now?"

"We start a fresh as l a family!" I said blankly.

I wanted my family i wanted not experience emotional pain ever again but an eye for an eye as they say.

I looked out the window bnot knowing when I'll ever return to America but at this moment all i wanted was to forget it.

I will be back but I won't be the same!

I promise.

The end of Insecurely confident part I.

www.ingramcontent.com/pod-product-compliance
Lightning Source LLC
Chambersburg PA
CBHW072149070526
44585CB00015B/1066